The Industrial
Buying Decision

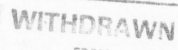

The Industrial Buying Decision

Implications for the sales
approach in industrial marketing

Gordon T. BRAND
B.Sc. (Econ)., Cert. I.T.P. (Harvard),
M.Inst.M

London
Cassell/Associated Business Programmes

Published by
Associated/Business Programmes Ltd.
17 Buckingham Gate, London S.W.1

Distributed by
Cassell and Co., Ltd.
35 Red Lion Square
London WC1

First Published 1972

*This book has been set in Times New Roman type, printed in Great Britain
on antique wove paper by Anchor Press, and
bound by Wm. Brendon, both of Tiptree, Essex*

ISBN 0 304 29078 5

039653

Contents

Foreword

The preoccupation of industrial marketers with the concepts and techniques of marketing and the belief, overt or covert, that marketing and industrial buying were two totally dissimilar activities with largely opposed interests manœuvring for the best possible posture, led to an oversimplified view of industrial buying. In the beginning, it might be said, there was just the buyer or the purchasing officer. It was only necessary to get him to say 'yes' and the marketing task was complete. Thus, marketing evolved ever more complex and subtle ways of obtaining an affirmative answer from the buyer but in a complete intellectual vacuum so far as an understanding of buying was concerned. This was partly caused by the belief, carried over from consumer goods purchasing, that the buyer was in essence the decision-maker and that within his budget he had freedom to commit the company. It took some time to appreciate that buying for resale and buying for own use or added value had dimensions unknown in the consumer goods field.

In every buying situation three factors needed to be known by the seller if there was to be any degree of precision in industrial marketing:

who buys—the composition of the DMU (decision-making unit); who within the company influences contracting decisions?

how do they buy—the buying process, incremental decisions not 'moment of truth'?

why do they buy—rational and irrational factors impacting on decisions?

Marketing literature and marketing teaching in the 1950s and early 1960s gives no indication of the subtle configurations and interplay of purchasing activities and motivations. Marketing men's preoccupation with the tools produced the very product orientation they denounced within industry.

It was this situation which, in 1965, encouraged The Institute of Marketing and Industrial Market Research Limited to jointly sponsor and conduct a survey to probe the first of the factors—'who buys'. The results of the research, published in 1967 under the title *How British Industry Buys*, proved beyond doubt that a typical DMU consists of three or more persons, some perhaps not even within the buying company, for example, architects, consultants, and customers, thus destroying for all time the shibboleth that the industrial purchasing officer, important as he is, is the sole arbiter in an industrial buying decision. The study also shows how frequently salesmen are misrouted and misdirected, and how frequently sales literature either fails to reach its target or conveys the wrong type of information relative to the DMU member's authority and interest.

The decision was taken in 1971 by The Institute of Marketing and Industrial Market Research Limited to update this study. Preliminary work showed at once that it would be far more valuable to probe actual decisions than to quantify the buying activity since it was considered that the earlier findings had adequately described a situation which had not changed significantly in the intervening period. Moreover, the work of the Marketing Science Institute in the USA, in the period since *How British Industry Buys* had thrown new and important light on the second factor—'how do they buy'. The MSI work destroyed as effectively the myth of the 'moment of truth' decisions as *How British Industry Buys* destroyed that of the single decision-maker. It was, however, a combination of the Marketing Science Institute's and Industrial Market Research Limited's work that provided the basic idea for this book. In the simplest terms the book sets out the results of probing deeply into what businessmen do as opposed to what they say they do; thus, this study builds on the previous work and, hopefully, will extend the reader's knowledge of buying and its interface with marketing.

Its purpose, however, is evangelical as well as informative. The unreal dichotomy between marketing and buying has to be destroyed intellectually and emotionally if marketing is to be purposeful and efficient. Waste in marketing, were it only quantifiable, would, it is suspected, be of astronomic proportions. There are the problems of inadequate advertising, mis-directed PR, expensive, over-elaborate and wasteful catalogues, abortive journeys and sales visits, junk direct mail; also the days and weeks of detailed planning, the operating and monitoring of complex marketing strategies which are doomed from the outset to failure or at best to limited success because of the lack of understanding of buying. No-one today thinks that selling and salesmen are the same as marketing and the marketing man. It should be equally obvious that buying is just one element, albeit a vital one, in a firm's operations, and the buyer is one element in the activity 'mix' just as the salesman is one element in the marketing 'mix'. This appreciation is a necessary pre-condition of successful marketing.

The needs of the buyer and the needs of the seller are not necessarily opposed nor are they necessarily contiguous. Good marketing and good purchasing start on the basis that they are two sides of a single activity directed to satisfying not only the needs of the seller but also those of the buyer.

Against this background it was natural to turn to Gordon T. Brand to lead the research project and to write up the results since he, when Head of Research at Industrial Market Research Limited, devised and carried out the fieldwork and analysis for the original study *How British Industry Buys*. Moreover, he subsequently studied buying and selling techniques in industrial markets at the Harvard Business School and was therefore in a position not only to compare the state of the art in Britain and the USA but also to utilise the latest American research. As principal lecturer in marketing at the School of Management, Bristol Polytechnic, Gordon Brand was in an excellent position to obtain the co-operation of industry for this more detailed study.

The Institute of Marketing and Industrial Market Research Limited wish to place on record their appreciation of the work of all involved in the study, particularly the many industrialists who gave freely of their time to provide the necessary information. The study was devised by many people but in particular we would like to acknowledge the work of David Jamieson of Industrial Market Research Limited who, with Gordon Brand, developed the objectives and basic methodology. The major effort of supervising, conducting, and analysing the fieldwork, and writing and preparing the manuscript for publication was that of Gordon Brand, and The Institute of Marketing and Industrial Market Research Limited freely acknowledge their debt to him for his meticulous work, patience, and never failing good humour even under the impact of much conflicting if well meaning advice.

Sir John Hamilton
President
The Institute of Marketing

Aubrey Wilson
Managing Director
Industrial Market Research Limited

Author's Acknowledgement

The author wishes to thank the respondents, chief buyers, senior engineering staff, design, development and other key personnel in the firms co-operating with the survey. Thanks are also due to Industrial Market Research Ltd. and the Institute of Marketing for their encouragement and financial support and to the Department of Business Administration and Management Studies, Bristol Polytechnic for allowing a small but energetic group of postgraduate students to express their interest in industrial marketing by the very practical means of assisting with the field work of the survey. Finally, my thanks are due to my wife Daphne who suffered the disturbance and effort of typing the manuscript without too much complaint.

1

The Study of Industrial
Buyer Behaviour

The Need to Study Buyers

There is a well known expression that 'there is nothing new under the sun' and without doubt, such an expression can be applied to the need of the seller to study the behaviour of people likely to buy from him. Surely the successful Phoenician trader, the Roman potter, the owner of an Elizabethan playhouse, the Victorian entrepreneur, the stall holder in a street market, the head of market development at I.B.M., owe some of their success to their understanding of what their customers want of them as suppliers?

This traditional interest in buyer behaviour has become more formalised in recent decades as industrial and commercial units have grown in size and as competition for an expanding disposable income has increased.

To combat competition, companies have turned to marketing with the intention of seeking out which type of customer can be most profitably served, in preference to the less sophisticated objective of encouraging their salesmen to collect as many orders as possible from any and all types of customers. The marketing concept with its emphasis on the maximisation of profitability rather than sales volume requires a very close study of existing and potential customers to discern which market segments offer the best opportunities. A first stage application of marketing to a company's operations for example, can be witnessed in the simple analysis of customers by size of potential business and the consequent elimination of the smaller non-profitable accounts to permit greater concentration of available resources on 'VIP' customers.

More research is required to ascertain the type of products most likely to meet the current and future needs of the market but once the strategic decisions of segmentation and product specifications have been made, the efficiency of tactical marketing activities such as advertising, personal representation technical advice and service provision will be improved if directed in accord with the knowledge of buying practices and buying influences. Consumer marketing research has developed largely from the information needs of advertising and sales management whereas industrial market research has concentrated in the past on major decision areas, reporting at Board level, for example, on the viability of a proposed entry into a new market or opportunities for a new technology. The tactical market information in industrial markets has frequently been left for the sales representative to collect through his regular and direct contact with customers. Sufficient industrial market research expertise is now available, however, to obtain information on purchasing behaviour which can be used in the profitable deployment of industrial marketing effort to supplement the more specific knowledge of individual product requirements and administrative practices available to the sales representative through his regular contacts with buyers.

The Study of Industrial Purchasing Behaviour

A number of the reports and comments on various aspects of industrial purchasing behaviour published in recent years are reviewed in Chapter 7. With one or two important exceptions the majority of these studies have concentrated on the behaviour of the professional buyer but since the mid 1960's two key areas of research have emerged which have widened the approach to the subject. These two areas can be summarised:

● Industrial purchasing decisions are shared decisions subject to a variety of influences.
● Industrial purchasing is a process of problem solving spread over time.

These general statements, although acceptable as general descriptions, inevitably require some qualification if they are to be applied in practice to the known variety of industrial purchasing situations. In combination, however, they provide a useful approach to the fuller understanding of industrial purchasing behaviour.

The first full scale investigation in Britain of the shared purchasing decision process was the predecessor of the current study, similarly jointly sponsored by Industrial Market Research Ltd. and the Institute of Marketing, and published under the title *How British Industry Buys*.[1]

The main objective of the research was to quantify in different industry groupings the relationship between the variety of personnel jointly involved in the purchase of three types of industrial goods, namely, plant equipment, materials and components—a division first used in an industrial purchasing study by Duncan in the United States in 1940 and accepted since then as a useful classification of industrial goods.[2]

As with other studies before and since, the *How British Industry Buys* survey found different patterns of purchasing behaviour both between different industry groupings and also between different firms in the same industry grouping. A definite pattern emerged, however, across industry for three product classifications.

For industry as a whole, the personnel most concerned with purchasing were,

	Board
For Plant Equipment	Operating Management
	Production Engineers

	Buying Department
For Materials &	Design & Development
Components	Engineers
	Operating Management

The decision to buy was found to be shared by the above groups of specialists supported in different purchasing situations by other groups such as sales, research or maintenance, who, when acting together, are referred to as a Decision Making Unit or DMU.

The full value of the survey, which was essentially quantitative, can be obtained by a close study of the published tables which represent the analysis and summation of the completed mail questionnaires, returned by British industrial companies.

[1] *How British Industry Buys*, Hutchinson, London 1967.
[2] Duncan, D. J., *What Motivates Business Buyers*, Harvard Business Review 1940.

Table 1. How Industry Buys Plant Equipment

In industry personnel with these functions →
participate in the percentages indicated, at
these steps in the development of a purchase*

		Board (general management)	Operating management	Prod. engineering	Des. & dev. engineering	Maint. engineering	Research	Buying	Finance	Sales	Others in company	Others outside company
1	Who is most likely to initiate projects leading to new equipment purchase for:											
a	Replacement of old equipment?	34	48	19	5	19	2	4	4	2	2	1
b	Expansion of capacity?	63	33	15	6	3	2	3	5	10	1	1
c	Change in process?	27	38	22	19	2	13	3	2	3	3	1
d	Production of a new product?	41	24	15	18	1	13	4	3	18	3	2
2	Who surveys alternatives and determines kind (not make) of equipment to be used?	15	43	30	23	8	4	4	1	1	4	1
3	Who specifies as to size, capacity, etc. of the equipment?	19	47	26	14	4	2	1	1	3	3	
4	Who surveys available makes or suppliers of the specified kind of equipment and chooses suppliers from whom to invite bids?	12	35	22	15	8	2	28	1	1	4	1
5	Who evaluates equipment offered by suppliers for their accord with specifications?	12	40	29	20	9	3	12	2		5	1
6	Who decides which supplier gets the order?	44	28	10	7	3		19	1	2	2	

Example: In industry generally in specifying size ann capacity of plant equipment production engineers in 26% of plants play more than an occasional role.

The extracts shown in Tables 1–3 show how the purchasing decision is shared for capital equipment, materials and components in industry as a whole.

In Table 1 Operating management are seen to make the major contribution to the decisions to purchase plant equipment although the Board in over 60 per cent of the plants surveyed are dominant in those decisions relating to plant for expansion of capacity. Maintenance engineering personnel figure in the replacement of old equipment but Buyers in only one fifth of the plants share in the decision as to which supplier gets the eventual order.

Table 2 shows that in the purchase of materials the Buyer plays more than an occasional role in taking advantage of price differentials, searching for suppliers and deciding which supplier gets the order in over half of the plants surveyed. The Board's involvement is minimal, although Design and Development and Operating Management contribute substantially to the eventual decision.

The decision making pattern for components is shown in Table 3 to be more evenly spread between Operating Management, Design and Development, Maintenance and Buying with the exception of the latter's deeper involvement in the search for suppliers and in price negotiations.

The Need for Further Research

The *How British Industry Buys* survey has opened up a broad cross industry view showing clearly that the buying decision is shared between members of a Decision Making Unit and that the Buyer or Purchasing Manager, although an important member of this Unit, is by no means the sole arbiter in the negotiations to purchase goods whether components, materials or capital equipment. Fully structured postal questionnaires, however, can only penetrate a certain level of information and the analysis of the data they provide raises questions which require further examination.

In components and materials, for example, the Buyer's influence on which supplier is to be awarded the order can be constrained by the original specifications prepared by design and technical personnel limiting the choice to one preferred and possibly more expensive supplier. In such a case who has the most influence? A traditional fear expressed by engineering or technically trained personnel is that of a Buyer who, overzealous in his desire to increase profitability through efficient purchasing, saves two pennies per thousand on a

Table 2. How Industry Buys Materials

		In industry personnel with these functions participate in the percentages indicated, at these steps in the development of a purchase*	Board (general management)	Operating management	Prod. engineering	Des. & dev. engineering	Maint. engineering	Research	Buying	Finance	Sales	Others in company	Others outside company
1		Who is most likely to initiate projects leading to purchase of material:											
	a	To take advantage of a price differential?	10	21	5	4	2	2	59	2	4	1	1
	b	For change in characteristics of an established product?	11	29	10	23	2	15	19		11	3	1
	c	As a result of a change in production process?	7	36	22	12	2	10	20	1	4	2	1
	d	For production of a new product?	15	25	10	20	1	13	16	1	11	2	1
2		Who surveys alternatives and determines kind (not make) of material to be used?	8	27	12	27	3	17	22	1	4	3	2
3		Who sets up specifications and standards to be met by the material?	6	25	12	31	3	20	10		5	3	3
4		Who surveys available makes or suppliers of the specified kind of material and chooses suppliers from whom to invite bids?	7	22	6	10	2	6	59	1	1	3	1
5		Who evaluates the materials offered by suppliers for their accord with specifications?	5	27	11	22	3	17	28	1	1	6	1
6		Who decides which supplier gets the order?	17	25	5	6	1	4	52	1	1	1	1

*Example: In industry in deciding which supplier of materials gets the order the buying department in 52% of plants plays more than an occasional role.

Table 3. How Industry Buys Components

	In industry generally personnel with these functions → participate in the percentages indicated, at these steps in the development of a purchase*	Board (general management)	Operating management	Prod. engineering	Des. & dev. engineering	Maint. engineering	Research	Buying	Finance	Sales	Others in company	Others outside company
1	Who is most likely to originate projects leading to purchase of a component part:											
a	To take advantage of a price differential?	4	20	7	8	7	5	44	1	2	1	
b	As a result of a change in design of an established product?	4	21	15	27	8	5	16		4	2	1
c	As a result of a change in production process?	3	28	29	16	7	5	14		2	2	
d	For production of a new product?	8	25	13	24	3	7	14		8	2	1
2	Who surveys alternatives and determines kind (not make) of component parts to be used?	3	24	18	31	9	8	16	1	2	3	1
3	Who specifies design and characteristics of the parts?	3	20	15	38	8	9	3		3	3	2
4	Who surveys available makes or suppliers of the specified kind of component parts and chooses suppliers from whom to invite bids?	4	20	10	15	7	4	43	1	1	2	
5	Who evaluates component parts submitted by suppliers to accord with specifications?	3	21	16	27	8	6	18		1	5	1
6	Who decides which supplier gets the order?	10	25	6	9	4	4	39	1	1	1	

*Example In industry generally in specifying design and characteristics of components design and development engineers in 38% of plants play more than an occasional role.

component used in assembly but indirectly causes delays in production costing thousands of pounds because the new component
cannot be handled so easily by the assemblers or alternatively incurs
the even greater cost of service personnel having to replace faulty
parts on the customer's premises.

Such a complaint can be countered by the experience of researchers
investigating the British market for high stability resistors. Circuit
design engineers were found to be specifying the relatively high cost
± 1 per cent tolerance resistor when a radically cheaper ± 2 per cent
or in some cases ± 5 per cent would have done the job just as well.
The reason given by the design engineers was that they were not
always sure of the exact tolerance requirements in every part of the
circuit but they knew that the high quality resistor would easily
suffice and was therefore 'safe' as a circuit recommendation.

In such a case of apparent over—specification by technical personnel, the Buyer would be making a contribution to company profits by
seeking general approval for the purchase of less accurate but
cheaper resistors. But before such a move could be made further
assessment of the situation was required to put the problem in
perspective. How many resistors, whether high or low stability were
needed? What was the cost of components and materials used in
relation to the value added by the skill of the circuit designers? Once
the newly designed equipment was accepted and components and
materials regularly ordered, what circumstances could lead to a
change in suppliers? Who would bring about such a change?

If it were found that a decision taken at an early buying stage
could restrict the choice of those concerned with the later stages of
the purchase, should marketing effort be directed at the technical
decision makers or at Board management who are also involved in
the early stages?

In those areas where the buyer is shown to have a reduced role in
the purchasing decision, for example, in capital plant, what are the factors which influence the other members of the Decision Making Unit
concerned? What is the impact of marketing personnel of potential
suppliers in the early stages of the purchase? What are the implications of the rather sweeping statement that industrial goods are
bought rather than sold?

Not Only Who But When?

It was the discussion of these types of questions with marketing and purchasing executives during training courses and consultancy assignments that revealed many gaps in the knowledge of industrial purchasing processes and indicated the need for more qualitative research which could be used to supplement the quantitative results of the *How British Industry Buys* survey. It became clear that any new research should be extended to include not only *WHO* was involved in the decision process but also *WHEN* they were involved and what factors influenced the decisions made.

A further reason was that although recent research evidence has clearly shown the Buyer as only one of the members of the Decision Making Unit, and on occasion, playing a very minor role indeed it was impossible to ignore the increasingly sophisticated techniques available to buying departments such as Value Analysis, Economic Order, Quantity and Supplier Evaluation Systems. The paper published by the Ford Motor Company on the objectives and policies of the company's purchasing, department (reproduced in Appendix C) epitomizes the professional approach to the subject.

Members of the Institute of Purchasing and Supply have long been able to claim evidence of the contribution of their efforts to company profitability[3] and in the recent years of declining profit margins these claims have reached a more favourably disposed audience at general management level with the result that the purchasing and supply function has gained increasing recognition as a key profit centre in its own right.

Such recognition has always been present where relatively little value is added in manufacture and where a large percentage of the sale price of a product is the cost of raw materials bought in, but as can be seen in Table 4 purchases of all types form a large part of the total operations in the majority of industries.

Savings in purchasing costs are far easier to calculate than they are to obtain in reality. Nevertheless any strengthening of the purchasing function in order to realize the full profit potential in buying would need to be matched by an equivalent improvement in the marketing efficiency of companies when acting in their role as suppliers, if the profitability of the whole enterprise is to be maintained or increased.

[3] Alexander, J. O. M., 'The Role of the Supplies Function in Management', *Purchasing Journal*, London, November 1969.

TABLE 4

PURCHASES AS A PERCENTAGE OF SALES REVENUE

Standard Industrial Classification	Sales Goods Produced	Purchases for Production	Purchases as % of Sales
	£ million	£ million	
Metal Manufacture	4117	2781	68
Vehicles	4347	2961	68
Leather Goods	207	131	63
Chemicals	3452	2021	59
Food, Drink & Tobacco	7806	4639	59
Textiles	2617	1548	59
Timber & Furniture	1253	732	58
Electrical Engineering	3317	1920	58
Metal Goods	2509	1427	57
Mechanical Engineering	4338	2380	55
Clothing & Footwear	1120	599	53
Other Manufacture	1354	721	53
Instruments	587	293	50
Shipbuilding	539	266	49
Paper & Printing	2817	1250	44
	40380	23669	59

Source: Provisional results; Census of Production 1970, *Trade and Industry*, London, 23rd December, 1971.

The Research Approach

The second and more recent view of industrial purchasing as a process of problem solving spread over time provided an avenue of approach for a second stage research project which would probe the apparent paradox of Buyers having a relatively reduced share of key decision making at a time when clearly the purchasing function is increasing its status within the hierarchy of company management. In 1967, the American Marketing Science Institute published the results of a study by Patrick Robinson and Charles Faris into the purchasing processes of three companies identified as Companies Able, Baker and Charlie.[4] The work began on Company Able, on

[4] Robinson, P. J. and Faris, C. W., with contributions by Yoram Wind, *Industrial Buying and Creative Marketing*, Allyn & Bacon, Boston 1967.

purchases classified into three distinct types: capital goods; parts and materials; and maintenance, repair and operating supplies; but as work progressed the authors report

'it became increasingly apparent that the type of product was not clearly so important as the particular circumstances of the purchase in affecting patterns of procurement. The situation of the buyer with regard to information and experience was far more significant and consistent in explaining his buying behaviour and the procedures he followed in the procurement process.'

By the end of their survey, Robinson and Faris had refined all purchasing situations to three fundamentally distinct situations, described as New Task—Modified Rebuy—Straight Rebuy.

Full definitions of these classifications are given in Appendix D, but in brief, differences were found between the buying process for products being purchased for the first time; those where a change in product or supplier took place; and for regular purchases of the same product.

These three purchasing tasks were set against a framework of the purchasing process, beginning with the anticipation or recognition of a problem through to performance feedback and evaluation (*Figure 1*).

The analysis of the purchasing processes of the three tasks provided a useful framework for research carried out at far greater depth than previous studies made in Britain.

Approaches were made to 60 companies and organisations each employing over 250 personnel. Of these, 43 gave permission for a researcher to trace the purchasing decisions relating to three or more specific products and to interview executives involved in that process. In all, a total of 232 semi-structured personal interviews were conducted followed by a further 20 unstructured interviews with industrial sales and marketing managers to discuss the findings and their application to industrial marketing. More details of the research method, including the distribution of the interviews between industry classifications are given in Appendix A, page 110.

A key objective of the field research was to study the industrial purchasing process over time. Previous surveys had confirmed that the purchasing decision is shared between members of the Decision Making Unit but when this information is applied to the day-to-day task of selling to industry, the need for a further dimension becomes apparent—that of different degrees of involvement by different decision makers at different stages of the purchasing process.

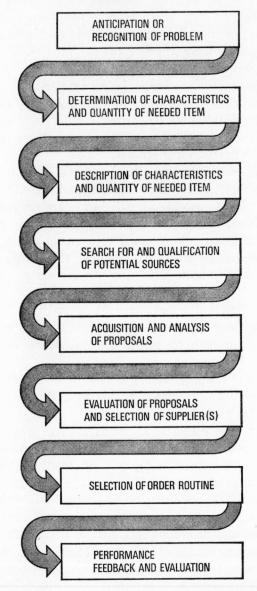

Figure 1 Stages in the process of purchasing industrial goods

Layout of the Book

A management summary in Chapter 2 provides an over-all view of the scope of the book, a summary of the main conclusions arising from the inquiries made and the implications of these conclusions for industrial marketing management.

The object of the book has been to increase the information available to industrial marketers by tracing a series of typical purchasing processes in a variety of industries and in a number of different companies within those industries.

In Chapters 3, 4 and 5 specific examples of purchasing decision processes are examined. Cases are presented in which purchases are followed from their source right through to the eventual placement of an order and the evaluation of the goods supplied. The behaviour of key members of the Decision Making Unit is reported and assessments made of their influence on the ultimate decision to purchase. In Chapter 6 these members of the DMU are examined in greater depth.

Chapter 7 contains a review of previous research into industrial purchasing and commentaries on its relevance to the day-to-day activities of the marketing practitioner. Finally, in Chapter 8 the implications of the research sponsored by Industrial Market Research Ltd. and the Institute of Marketing are related to the regular situations encountered by the industrial sales representative in his contact with buyers and other decision making members of customer organisations.

2

Management Summary

Direct sales representation has traditionally provided the manufacturer of industrial goods with a great deal of information as to his customer's needs. Face to face encounter between representative and buyer permits detailed discussion of technical specifications, delivery requirements, price and conditions of after sales service.

This clear, two-way channel of communication between producer and user, uncluttered by the needs of wholesalers and the reactions of retailers has for long supported the rationalisation that the behaviour of industrial buyers requires less attention than that of remote and fickle private consumers.

Conditions change, however. Market structures become more complex; companies grow both as suppliers and as customers; the risks of decision taking get bigger with the increasing cost of new product development and the need to commit large resources many years ahead.

The growth of professional industrial marketing research services during the last decade is proof of the value to management of the opportunity to stand back from the day-to-day contact with customers for an independent and systematic view of market trends, future product needs and profitable direction of promotional resources.

Supplementing, and in some instances, pre-dating the service of formally constituted industrial marketing research services tuned mainly to the particular problems of individual companies, there have been a number of rather less systematic surveys and probings of how industry goes about the task of buying in goods and supplies.

A great deal of this research effort has been directed at an attempt to solve the continuing argument as to whether industrial buyers are rational or irrational. As more and more evidence was provided of both rational and irrational actions, it became clear that to progress further, research should be conducted on a broader front moving away from the studies of designated Buyers or Purchasing Officers, to the entire process of buying within company organisation.

The acceptance of the Buyer as only one of a group of executives or Decision Making Unit (DMU) involved in the decision to purchase plant equipment, materials and components, brought the research effort nearer to the every-day problems of the industrial marketing practitioner faced with the task of reaching a number of technical, financial and commercial personnel operating at different levels of management and, at times, inaccessible to the sales engineer or representative.

Further research was required, however, to unravel the apparent paradox of the increasing acceptance of the DMU principle of shared decision taking in industrial purchasing which reduces the relative importance of the designated Buyer at a time when the skill and professionalism of purchasing was gaining more recognition in company management.

The Findings of the Current Research

Industrial purchasing can be viewed as a process of problem solving which extends from the early recognition of the problem through stages of fluctuating levels of activity until the eventual placing of an order. The composition of the Decision Making Unit and the extent of its involvement in the decision making process varies with a number of conditions and situations relating to the purchase. These include the degree of innovation and change proposed, technical complexity, the essentiality of the product in question, its cost, the status of the buyer, the number of potential suppliers and the market position of the purchasing firm.

Although these many variations can be found, a high degree of uniformity exists in the way personnel in manufacturing industry approach the acquisition of products that have not been purchased before, those purchased as repeat items and those which involve the change from a regular to a new supplier.

The current research has shown that the 'task' approach is applicable across a wide range of manufacturing industries. Looking at purchases, not from the point of the view of the manufacturing supplier as types of goods with certain technical characteristics, but from the view of the customer company which has to buy in supplies in different situations to continue in business, provides a fresh practical approach with important implications for industrial marketing management and for those responsible for the selling effort in particular.

In the new purchase situation, regardless of whether the product being purchased is plant equipment, materials or components, the key decisions are made in the early stages of the purchase largely by technical personnel.

The origin of the need to purchase may be a policy decision of the Board or of its General Management, but the details of technical specifications required or the supplier to be selected are promptly delegated.

Those responsible, in the early stages of the purchase for deciding what to buy lack technical information and as industrial purchasing is a process of progressive decision making, decisions taken at the early stages greatly influence the eventual selection of the preferred supplier. The potential supplier who provides information in a form suited to the needs of the purchasing groups' problem solving activities has a good opportunity of influencing the final purchasing decision in his favour. In spite of this, the sales and marketing influence of potential suppliers is frequently missing from the early stages of a new purchase decision.

Buyers are also largely absent from the decision taking process until a technical solution to the problem has been found, although the influence of the purchasing department on new purchase decisions is expected to grow with the increasing recognition given by senior management to the profit potential of the overall supplies function.

The popular interpretation of the DMU concept, which 'cuts the Buyer down to size', may lead to a misunderstanding of his role when existing suppliers are dropped in favour of new ones. Although the Buyer is only one of many contributing to the new purchase decision, the research findings show that he is likely to be the main instigator and decision taker when one source of repeat purchases is being changed for another, normally improved, source. The Buyer can be seen at his most active during this type of purchase decision.

Search and Selection of Suppliers

Restrictions on time and money limit the search by purchasing companies for new suppliers, but thorough checks are normally made to ensure the viability of the companies selected.

A further reason for inertia in supplier selection is that all purchasing can be viewed as a form of risk taking and any change may involve risk. To be successful, a new supplier to a company must reduce the feelings of risk associated with his selection.

The members of the Decision Making Unit who need to be assured of the absence of serious risk include not only those who take actions which direct the purchase through its various stages to its ultimate conclusion, but also those who can be termed 'decision influencers'. An important decision influencer may be someone outside the customer company, such as a consultant engineer advising on the type of boiler to be used in a heating installation. This engineer is easily identifiable as a DMU member and can be approached by the sales representative as such.

A less obvious, but highly respected decision influencer is the professional colleague in an associate or even competitor company, whose advice is sought by the purchasing company on new sources of supply and the evaluation of new suppliers.

These outside influencers form an important part of the Decision Making Unit frequently unrecognised in previous cross-industry research into industrial purchasing behaviour.

The senior general management or Board members of the DMU can be more correctly described as decision influencers rather than decision takers in the purchasing of industrial goods. Although many purchases would not take place without their indirect support, they are not usually present when the details on which key purchasing decisions are taken are discussed.

Implication for Industrial Selling

Each of the attributes considered important for the industrial sales representative can be improved in the light of the increasing knowledge of industrial purchasing behaviour.

The managers responsible for the sales activity of their companies should recognise the adaptability required of the salesman which goes far beyond the realisation that products are different and that different customer personnel influence the buying decision.

Adaptability in this context includes the flexibility vital to the salesman confronted by changes in interest and motivation of his customers, but it also embraces the ability to recognise what triggers off interest in a new purchase; a change in a repeat purchase pattern; or the importance of anticipating and preventing any change once listed as a preferred supplier.

Implications for Industrial Marketing Management

Overall, the research findings draw attention to the fact that industrial purchasing and industrial selling are simply two sides of the same coin. They represent not a process of confrontation but a close inter-relationship which, to be profitable to both sides, requires from the supplier a close attention to internal and environmental problems faced by customers and from the purchaser, an invitation to partici-pate early in company problem solving and the prospect of continuing profitability from that participation.

3

Purchasing for the First Time

All types of industrial purchases have their origins in the existence
of problems which can only be solved by obtaining goods or services
from an outside supplier. When a problem is recognised for the first
time, the decision to buy may be preceded by a 'make or buy' study
to investigate the technical and economic feasibility of meeting the
requirement from resources inside the company or buying in the
finished article or complete service—but in either case purchases will
result.

The 'new task' or first time purchases traced in the current research
fall into two broad classifications, namely those arising from events
external to the purchasing company and those arising from internal
events.

External v. Internal Motivation

Purchases most easily recognised as first time purchases are those
triggered off by events occurring in the environment in which the
company is operating. Some of the reactions to these events are
controllable, such as the decision to allocate resources to exploit a
market opportunity; others are uncontrollable, perhaps the forced
reaction to competition from a new technology or the legal obligation
to instal effluent treating equipment.

An example of internal motivation is the replacement of worn-out
equipment which becomes a new, first-time purchase when the need
to replace provides the opportunity for a fresh look at the problem
posed.

These cases which follow, have been drawn from the information collected during the field survey. In some instances, the exact circumstances of the purchase have been altered to ensure anonymity for the respondent firms but none of these change the basic principles of the decision making processes being described.

New Purchase Case Examples

Company A: Electrical Industry:
Purchase of Mould for Diode Manufacture

RECOGNITION
OF NEED TO
PURCHASE

Company *A*, well established in the electro-mechanical market had capital available from the sale of a substantial shareholding in another company. The BOARD met to discuss diversification as a means of securing growth and profitable employment of capital available. New product suggestions were discussed and the recommendation of the SALES DIRECTOR to enter the expanding market for silicon diodes accepted.

The PRODUCTION MANAGER was directed to set up facilities for the manufacture of silicon diodes.

DETERMINATION
OF PRODUCT
CHARACTERISTICS

SALES AND PRODUCTION ENGINEERING advised the PRODUCTION MANAGER on the quantities and specifications of diodes required, the most economic use of manufacturing space and production personnel. From this information it was decided that a mould with facility for x number of impressions should be obtained.

DESCRIPTION
OF PRODUCT
CHARACTERISTICS

The PRODUCTION MANAGER gave PRODUCTION EQUIPMENT ENGINEERING full details of the manufacturing requirement, requesting provision of suitable equipment

SEARCH FOR
POTENTIAL
SUPPLIERS

The PRODUCTION EQUIPMENT ENGINEERS assessed the request from the Production Dept., and concluded three possible procedures:

(a) Develop and manufacture own mould at Company *A*

(b) Purchase from United States supplier

(c) Purchase from British supplier.

Possibility (a) was rejected taking into account work load and technical skills available. The known United States supplier was to be approached for quotation and British suppliers to be sought.

QUALIFICATION
OF POTENTIAL
SUPPLIERS

The PRODUCTION EQUIPMENT ENGINEERS with some assistance from PURCHASING located three possible British suppliers. Each of the three potential British suppliers were visited by PRODUCTION EQUIPMENT ENGINEERS with the prime objective of investigating and assessing manufacturing facilities. In particular the quality of the chrome plating of the mould was deemed critical for high performance. One potential supplier, who intended to sub-contract the chrome plating work, refused to name the sub-contractor involved.

The United States supplier had a well established reputation for technical excellence and contact with the company's United Kingdom representative was considered to be sufficient at this stage. The representative confirmed that his company would be pleased to quote for the order.

ACQUISITION AND
ANALYSIS OF
PROPOSALS

The PRODUCTION EQUIPMENT ENGINEERS produced a final specification and requested the BUYER to seek quotations from the potential United States and British suppliers. The quotation received offered prices ranging from £7,500 from the US company to £4,650 to £3,500 from the British companies.

EVALUATION OF
PROPOSALS

SALES REPRESENTATIVES of the companies asked to quote were invited to visit the PRODUCTION EQUIPMENT ENGINEERS for detailed discussions on the technical aspects of the quotations. The United States company offered the longest delivery and the highest price. The UK supplier No. 1 with the highest price offered 6 months delivery; UK supplier No. 2, a medium price with 6 months delivery and UK supplier No. 3 the lowest price and 3 months delivery. The latter was still reluctant to reveal his subcontract arrangements.

The PRODUCTION EQUIPMENT ENGINEERS recommended UK supplier No. 2.

SELECTION OF
SUPPLIER

The PRODUCTION MANAGER called a meeting of PRODUCTION EQUIPMENT ENGINEERS, PRODUCTION ENGINEERS and the BUYER to discuss the quotations and recommendations. The recommendation to reject the United States quotation was endorsed not only on grounds of price but also on the possibility of the need to chase delivery and seek technical assistance after installation. The chain of contact from the United States through the UK representative was considered to be too long. The recommendation of UK supplier No. 2 was queried by the PRODUCTION MANAGER. The company had been operating the United Kingdom for only six months and the staff established here would still require some technical assistance from the United States. He foresaw delays in delivery. The third British supplier was rejected as the PRODUCTION EQUIPMENT ENGINEERS had no confidence in that company's ability to manufacture a technically acceptable product. The PRODUCTION MANAGER selected UK supplier No. 1.

SELECTION OF ORDER ROUTINE

The SALES DIRECTOR of the selected supplier was invited to Company *A* by the BUYER. Intense haggling ensued over delivery dates and a severe penalty clause for late delivery insisted upon. This was finally agreed by the supplier.

PERFORMANCE FEEDBACK AND EVALUATION

The rigorous conditions insisted upon by the BUYER ensured delivery by the agreed date and the technical service on installation was found to be satisfactory. No formal system existed in Company *A* for the evaluation of purchases and suppliers of this type, but if production requirements for diodes expand a further mould would be purchased and the favourable performance of supplier No. 1 would be taken into account in the future.

Company B: Machinery Manufacture: Purchase of Components

RECOGNITION OF NEED TO PURCHASE

This case concerns a company which manufactures machinery for the clothing industry. Feedback from the SALES FORCE, later confirmed by group MARKETING RESEARCH, revealed a market need for a completely new type of machine. The GENERAL MANAGER after further discussion with the SALES MANAGER decided to enter the new market.

Key company personnel were asked to investigate the technical problems and possibilities arising from the decision, in principle, of market entry.

DETERMINATION OF PRODUCT CHARACTERISTICS

The GENERAL MANAGER called a meeting of the SALES MANAGER, PRODUCTION MANAGER, RESEARCH & DEVELOPMENT and DESIGN personnel to discuss whether the machine should be manufactured by the company or bought in for re-sale. It was decided to design and manufacture a new machine to meet specified market requirements.

DESCRIPTION OF
PRODUCT
CHARACTERISTICS

There was a need to purchase many parts for the proposed machine but the researchers selected for further study a decision, to approach the hydraulic, pneumatic and associated electrical and electronic component problems through the purchase of a 'hydraulic package deal'. Involved in the decision were VALUE ENGINEERING, R & D, DESIGN and PRO-DUCTION who had become aware of the package deal approach through contact with engineers in associated companies in the Group and through articles in technical journals.

It was decided to contact potential suppliers of the hydraulic package deal.

SEARCH FOR
POTENTIAL
SUPPLIERS AND
ASSESSING THEIR
QUALIFICATIONS

One company, Potential Supplier 1, which had supplied an associate company, was already known to the R & D and DESIGN personnel and names of other market leaders were confirmed with PURCHASING. SALES REPRESENTATIVES were invited to call and preliminary contact made with engineering personnel of the potential suppliers. At the request of DESIGN, the BUYER invited formal quotations from four potential suppliers.

EVALUATION OF
PROPOSALS

The quotations received were jointly evaluated by all the members of the Decision Making Unit referred to in the various stages above with the exception of the General Manager who had withdrawn from the purchasing process after the decision, at stage 2, to manufacture the machine. Evaluation included such topics as design, quality and price in relation to the anticipated life of the machine and delivery. Each of the four suppliers who had quoted were considered to be technically proficient and there was little variation in the price of the package (approximately £5,000).

SELECTION OF
SUPPLIER

RESEARCH AND DEVELOPMENT and the BUYER were responsible for the final selection of the supplier, taking into account the recommendations and comments of the other departments mentioned. In summary, there was little technical disagreement. All four potential companies had produced quotations which showed sufficient understanding of the purchasing company's technical requirements. Some preference was shown for Potential Supplier No. 1, whose technical SALES REPRESENTATIVES had been particularly helpful when first contacted and in retrospect were seen to be more persistent than the remaining three potential suppliers. The BUYER endorsed the technical preference for Supplier No. 1 as he was concerned with the relatively short time available for the design and manufacture of the machine. The delivery times quoted would meet the production schedule but he had no way of assessing how the potential suppliers would keep their promises. In the case of Supplier No. 1, however, he had been able to discuss their performance with colleagues in the associated company and they had had no delivery problems with their previous purchases of similar equipment. Potential Supplier No. 1 was given the order for the 'hydraulic package deal'.

SELECTION OF
ORDER
ROUTINE

Once the selection had been made the final arrangements for purchasing and delivery were left to the BUYER and his department working in close relations with the STOCK CONTROLLER.

PERFORMANCE
FEEDBACK AND
EVALUATION

Feedback on supplier performance was collected from PRODUCTION and ASSEMBLY, the TESTING BAY, SALES, CUSTOMER and the SERVICE DEPARTMENT. Very little trouble had been encountered in getting the Supplier to replace any faulty items in the hydraulic equipment.

Company C: Food Industry:
Purchase of Raw Material

RECOGNITION OF
NEED TO
PURCHASE

By following the latest technical developments in the industry, senior DEVELOPMENT LABORATORY staff had become aware of the availability of an edible casing material which they considered could be usefully incorporated into the company's products.

DESCRIPTION OF
PRODUCT
CHARACTERISTICS

The details of the specification of the edible casing required were prepared by the DEVELOPMENT LABORATORY staff. This information was then passed to the BUYER and his department.

SEARCH FOR
POTENTIAL
SUPPLIERS

As the edible casing had not been purchased before the BUYER went through his references of possible suppliers and began to make inquiries by telephone.

The companies contacted were not, in fact, suppliers of the casing but names were obtained from these trade contacts of two potential suppliers.

QUALIFICATION OF POTENTIAL SUPPLIERS

Samples were obtained from both potential suppliers by post. No supplier representative called but as this was a new purchase the BUYER expected a representative to call eventually.

The samples were tested by the DEVELOPMENT LABORATORY staff and both passed as meeting the specification required.

EVALUATING OF PROPOSALS AND SELECTION OF SUPPLIER

Once the quality of the edible casings had been cleared, the DEVELOPMENT LABORATORY personnel withdrew from the purchasing process leaving the final selection to the BUYER. There was little difference in the prices quoted by the two potential suppliers but one was able to quote immediate delivery. As the development work was completed the manufacture of the new food product could start as soon as a regular supply of casings was obtained. The BUYER selected the supplier offering immediate delivery.

SELECTION OF ORDER ROUTINE AND PERFORMANCE FEEDBACK

Details of the order routine were negotiated by the BUYER with the supplying company concerned. The evaluations of supplier performance regarding delivery and price of the edible casings would now become part of the regular purchasing process for repeat orders.

Although Potential Supplier No. 2 had not been chosen because of the poor delivery offered, regular details of this alternative company's prices and delivery terms were obtained so that a performance of the current supplier could be reviewed in these respects. A favourable change in price would be sufficient for the BUYER to switch from an existing to an alternative supplier, without reference to the DEVELOPMENT personnel, although all raw material purchases would be tested as a routine procedure before being used in food production.

Technical SALES REPRESENTATIVES called occasionally but it had been possible for the BUYER to deal with some suppliers for years by post and telephone without meeting any of their sales or marketing staff. This was not considered to be abnormal by the BUYER interviewed.

Company D: Electric Motor Industry:
New Roller Bearing

RECOGNITION OF THE NEED TO PURCHASE	The DESIGN PERSONNEL in their work on the preparation of an improved electric motor decided that a new type of roller bearing, not used in previous designs, would have to be purchased.
DETERMINATION OF PRODUCT CHARACTERISTICS AND SEARCH FOR POTENTIAL SUPPLIERS	The technical problem to be solved determined the size and type of bearing required and the DESIGN personnel invited technical SALES REPRESENTATIVES from well known potential suppliers to assist them in their problem solving.

The BUYER and his department were involved in providing a full list of potential suppliers and twenty names were provided. A number of the firms listed were not considered seriously as potential suppliers and contact was made with eight of the original twenty including companies in Germany, France and Japan.

QUALIFICATION OF POTENTIAL SUPPLIERS AND ANALYSIS OF PROPOSALS	The assessment and evaluation of potential suppliers was shared by DESIGN and the BUYER. The final specification had been the responsibility of DESIGN and test samples had been obtained from eight potential suppliers. These samples were assessed for time— running, noise and reliability and technical performance in general.

These technical results were combined with the assessment of the BUYER based on his experience of previous dealings with the companies concerned, prices quoted and their reputation for delivery and customer relations.

SELECTION OF SUPPLIER	The elimination of unsuccessful potential suppliers had begun when the formal quotations were received by the BUYER but further discussions took place between the BUYER and DESIGN ENGINEERS. The screening for technical performance had produced two preferred suppliers and the BUYER selected the company with the better commercial reputation.

Company E: Engineering Industry:
Purchase of New Conveyor

RECOGNITION OF NEED TO PURCHASE	This purchase was triggered off by the comment and recommendations of the PLANT MAINTENANCE Manager who reported the increasing cost of maintaining a conveyor line. The ENGINEERING Dept. were informed

and a study made of how the line could be improved.

The company in question is a subsidiary of a large group and joint meetings are held of engineers at all the member plants at which common engineering problems are discussed. At one of these meetings the CHIEF ENGINEER at the plant being researched had heard of a novel form of conveyor equipment which had been installed successfully elsewhere in the company.

DETERMINATION
OF PRODUCT
CHARACTERISTICS

A meeting was held by the ENGINEERING Department and PLANT MAINTENANCE to discuss the technical solution of the conveyor problem. The CHIEF ENGINEER introduced the topic of the new patented conveyor system and it was agreed that if such a system were incorporated in the production line it would both solve the replacement of the old conveyor and shorten the line thus providing more space.

DESCRIPTION OF
PRODUCT
CHARACTERISTICS

The manufacturer of the new conveyor system was invited to put forward a detailed recommendation for the solution of the conveyor problem which would incorporate his new equipment.

SEARCH FOR
SUPPLIERS

No search for alternative suppliers was made as it was understood that the supplier already contacted had registered his design which was therefore 'unique'.

EVALUATION OF
PROPOSALS AND
SELECTION OF
SUPPLIER

The recommendations put forward by the one supplier invited to do so were found to be satisfactory by the CHIEF ENGINEER and approved by PLANT MAINTENANCE. The quotation was accepted by the CHIEF ENGINEER, and the overall approval for the purchase given by the AREA GENERAL MANAGER whose concern was not with the details of the purchase but only that the money to be spent was available within the budget allocated for capital equipment.

SELECTION OF
ORDER ROUTINE

The BUYER was not involved in this particular purchase for equipment until all the technical details had been approved and the supplier selected by the CHIEF ENGINEER. The BUYER's role therefore was the straightforward one of placing the order and ensuring that company rules regarding payment and responsibility for delivery and installation of the equipment were incorporated in the purchase agreement.

New Purchases:
Stages of the Purchasing Process

Recognition of the Need to Purchase

In the many new purchase situations studied, a variety of reasons were given by respondents explaining why the product or service involved was required in the first place and how arrangements were made to start the purchase process. In the new purchase decisions the companies concerned could be seen to be reacting to some external stimulus occasioned by a change in the environment or more simply to an internal stimulus such as the need to replace existing plant and machinery not functioning at maximum efficiency. Both of these situations are shown in the preceding examples.

The purchase of the mould (Company *A*) sprang from the deliberations of a Board of Directors faced with the task of maintaining and forcefully increasing growth and profitability in a period of re-organisation resulting from the sale of an interest in an associate company. The reasons for the sale which are not fully explained for reasons of confidentiality, could be viewed as the true source of the new purchase decision, but in effect the deliberations which led to the purchase began when the Board took upon themselves the task of matching the company's resources (now changed in terms of liquid financial assets) to market opportunities found in the external environment. The external stimulus is represented here in the expansion of the total demand for silicon diodes as recognised by the sales director.

In Company *B* the stimulus was again to be found outside the firm in the feedback from sales intelligence and marketing research which had reported a change in customer requirements. The Company's general management reacted to this information by calling for an

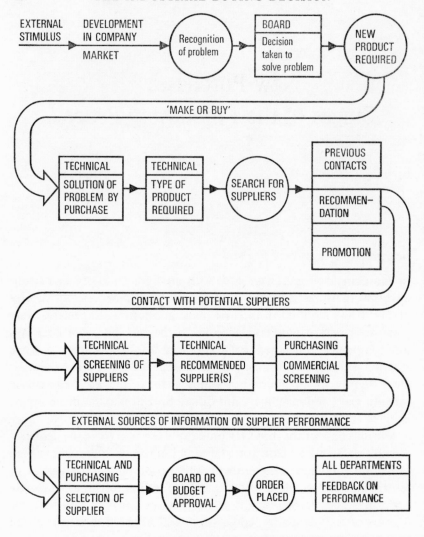

Figure 2 Purchasing a product new to the company

investigation into the feasibility of providing a suitable machine which would meet the changing needs of customers.

In the food industry example, Company *C*, was expanding by taking advantage of changing food preferences shown by the consuming public which in turn had their effects on the increased demand for edible casings. In Company *D*, the requirement for a new type of roller bearing was occasioned by the general external market pressures typical in a highly competitive industry, which create a continuous demand for improved technical performance. The manufacturers in the electric motor market will seek to differentiate themselves in the eyes of their customers by providing a better technical performance, better service or better prices than their many competitors.

In the last example Company *E*, the need for a new conveyor was first recognised by the Plant Maintenance Manager. The motivation for the purchase was entirely an internal matter with no external influence present until later stages of the decision process.

DMU Members Involved

Inevitably, the Board or general management will be involved when a company is about to redirect the allocation of resources in reaction to a change in its market environment. In the new purchase examples which stem from these changes, therefore, senior management are involved in the first stages of the process of acquisition but it would be wrong to conclude from this that the Board of the companies interviewed performed a key role in subsequent decisions regarding what type of product should be purchased to help implement their policies or indeed which supplier should eventually get the order. In the first four case examples the Board or senior management can be seen to be 'decision influencers' rather than decision makers. Without the influence of the top policy makers the new purchase would not have been required at all but once a decision had been taken to go ahead, for example to enter a new market, prepare a feasibility study or improve the product range, the task of what to buy and who to buy it from was immediately delegated to the relevant technical staff.

In the case of the conveyor purchase which was motivated by events internal to the company, the suggestion came from the Maintenance Department that the existing line should be replaced, but no action was taken to discuss what type of conveyor would be needed until the Chief Engineer had recognised the deficiency and had taken responsibility for the problem. A more senior influence was present in the form of an Area General Manager, acting as Financial Controller. Approval was required to release funds for the purchase, but his only role was to ensure that the Chief Engineer was not exceeding his budget for plant and equipment. He was not involved in any way with the decision of what equipment was to be purchased.

It would be naïve to suggest that the influence of Board policy will not extend, in any circumstance, to a decision as to which supplier gets to business. Examples were located during the research of reciprocal trading between a manufacturer of tyres and its fork-lift truck customer. In another case, metal extrusions were bought from a restricted list of two potential manufacturers 'sent down' once a year to the Purchasing Department by the Managing Director, but there was no evidence to suggest that such trading policies were made without regard to the technical performance of the product or its acceptability to user departments in the firm.

The truth surrounding informal reciprocal agreements or indeed the possibility of bribery could not be obtained by the research methods considered suitable for this enquiry. Those involved in the practical cut and thrust of industrial sales negotiations are in the best position to assess the extent to which unethical practices distort the buying procedures in their own particular business.

Determination of Product Characteristics

In the Buy phase framework presented by Robinson and Faris (page 22) separate stages are allocated to first, planning the type of product or service required and second, the preparation of detailed descriptions of what is to be purchased. In a number of new purchase situations such a distinction was found but in others the two stages were telescoped into one and sometimes joined with the search for suppliers.

In Company A, specific discussions took place during which the sales forecast for the new components was used to calculate the number of impressions required in the mould to be purchased. The implications of the potential sales figures on the rate of production were fully discussed with production personnel before an agreed manufacturing requirement was passed on to the production equipment department. It then became the duty of the production equipment personnel to find a supplier of a suitable mould.

In the clothing machinery Company B the implications of 'make or buy' preceded the decision which led to the need for the hydraulic components. In the food Company C, both stages were merged in the deliberations of the development chemists who worked out what was required from the new purchase and were then able to give a detailed specification to the purchasing department.

In the roller bearing example, however, the design engineers had been very much involved in the earlier policy decisions of product improvement. They also knew that the improved electric motor would require a high quality bearing but they were unable to complete their decisions as to the exact specification until a search had been made for suppliers who could assist them in these early design stages. In this case three stages were telescoped into one continuing operation.

In Company *E* the design for the conveyor system was not decided upon until after the eventual supplier had been called in to give his solution to the problem.

Importance of the Early Stages

It would be wrong to force the stages of these purchasing examples into the routine of a sequential straight jacket although the tasks referred to by Robinson and Faris have to be carried out in one order or another before a purchase can be made.

More important than the exact sequence, is the fact than the deliberations at these early stages tend to shape the outcome of the eventual purchase. When the representative of a potential supplier is called in to advise on design, performance or layout he is being given the opportunity to so influence the technical solution to the problem that those involved in the later stages of the purchase must approve of his company as the preferred supplier. If an engineer requests the purchase of an expensive proprietary product the purchasing department can ask him to explain why a known cheaper equivalent would not suffice, but when the engineers are requesting purchases to solve a problem not previously encountered in the company the opinions and recommendations of the 'outsider' are more likely to receive an attentive audience.

D.M.U. Members involved

A number of different personnel are involved in those stages of the purchasing process concerned with planning the type of the new product required and its detailed description. A relationship was found between production and production equipment personnel; between design and development and potential suppliers; between maintenance personnel and the chief engineer; and contributions to decisions were made by value analysis specialists. Titles, job functions and procedures vary in different companies but whatever the industry or type of product concerned and regardless of the organisation of individual companies within the industry, the DMU for the early 'problem solution' stages of a new purchase is restricted to technical personnel of one description or another. Purchasing staff and general management are significantly absent in the decision-making process although it does not follow that these non-technical members of the Decision Making Unit are unable to influence the purchase at some other stage.

Search for Potential Suppliers

The search for the supplier of a product or service not previously purchased takes place during any or all of the first four stages of the purchasing process. In Company A, the production and production equipment engineers were aware of the American manufacturer of high precision moulds and a senior engineering executive who had visited the American plant some two years earlier was available for consultation in the very early preparation for the project. The production equipment engineers had some difficulty in locating a British based supplier however and the planning of the new project had proceeded for some weeks before any contact could be made with technical representatives of known potential manufacturers.

In Company B, the technical decision to go ahead with a 'hydraulic package deal' was influenced by the design engineers' awareness, from conversations with colleagues in associated companies and from their reading of technical journals, that suppliers of such packages were in existence.

The Company C purchasing procedure fits more conveniently into the sequence of the Robinson and Faris buyphase sequence. The early development work was conducted before any search was made for potential suppliers. As this was a new requirement for the Company no obvious supplier was listed in the Purchasing Department and considerable effort was expended before the names of edible casing manufacturers were obtained.

A number of well known potential suppliers of roller bearings were invited to participate in the early design stages in the Company D example although the search for an even larger number of bearing manufacturers both national and international, continued throughout the development stage.

In Company E, the decisions to go ahead with the replacement of the ailing conveyor line were inextricably interwoven with the knowledge, imparted through intersite engineering meetings, that a particular manufacturer's system could provide a solution to the problem.

More important than the relative position of the 'search' stage in the buying process are perhaps the methods employed by manufacturers to effect the search. Greater variations exist in supplier search procedures than in any other facet of the purchasing process. The most sophisticated procedures were found in the process industries where one company's purchasing department had the use of a market researcher in group purchasing headquarters to investigate medium and long term sources of raw material supplies. At the other end of the search spectrum, companies were found to be basing their decisions on sources of supply on the valued opinions of colleagues in associated or even competitor companies.

Two common factors are present at the search stage regardless of the wide variations in the practices of individual companies. It is noticeable that:

- A high degree of preference is given to potential suppliers either known to personnel inside the purchasing company or to professional colleagues employed in other firms.
- The pressure of limited time between the decision to go ahead with the design of a new product and scheduled production date, contributes to a need to restrict the search to known companies rather than extend investigations in the expectation of a better purchase in terms of technical quality or price.

DMU Members Involved

The knowledge and advice of colleagues is a means of getting together a list of possible suppliers to approach, although advertising and technical journals are also regarded as important sources of supplier information. Direct mail is not considered to be a useful source of information on new suppliers unknown to the company.

The search for the potential suppliers of products new to the purchasing company is largely in the hands of the technical decision makers, but Purchasing departments are asked to assist by providing names of possible suppliers to be approached.

Qualifications of Potential Suppliers

Although the pressures of time limit the search for potential suppliers, a great deal of attention is given to the task of assessing the capabilities of the final short list of manufacturers requested to submit quotations.

A minimum of two production equipment engineers of Company *A* visited the premises of all three potential British suppliers to inspect manufacturing facilities and for detailed discussion with the suppliers' design staff.

A considerable amount of information on one of the four companies asked to quote for the hydraulic package was available to the design engineers of Company *B* from an associate company, but representatives from each of the companies on the short list called for a technical appraisal of the problem and to collect information on which to base their quotations. The type of business in the food company example, enabled the development chemists to evaluate the competence of the two suppliers located through the samples supplied. No sales representatives were expected and the communication between the purchasing company and potential supplier was effected by telephone and letter.

In Company *D* a technical assessment of competing products was possible, as for Company *C* through the testing of samples supplied. Supplementing these was an awareness of the reputation of the leading bearing manufacturers for research and development and known technical excellence in products similar to those under review.

As only one supplier was asked to quote for the conveyor system required by Company *E* the evaluation of that supplier was based, not by comparison with an alternative solution, but on the basis of the technical details put forward for consideration and on the recommendation of professional colleagues who were confident of the merits of the scheme proposed.

DMU Members Involved

The assessment of the qualification of manufacturers asked to quote for the supply of products new to the purchasing company is the responsibility of the technical members of the DMU. Purchasing staff require to be kept informed by both their technical colleagues and the representatives of potential suppliers of the progress and outcome of tests or other assessment activities but no instances were found of direct intervention at the pre-quotation stage.

Evaluation of Proposals and Selection of Supplier

A first stage evaluation takes place in the technical screening during the pre-quotation stages of the purchasing process but once the quotations have been received a second stage commercial evaluation is added to the technical. In Company *A*, the production equipment engineers, having examined in depth the design and manufacturing capabilities of the British based suppliers, submitted an unfavourable report on one, approved the remaining two but recommended one of these two as their preferred supplier. The Production Manager, however, who had been given direct responsibility by the Board for setting up the new line for the manufacture of the diodes was not satisfied with the assurances on delivery dates given by the preferred supplier.

As both possible suppliers had been passed on technical grounds, the Production Managers main concern was to ensure that there would be no delays in delivery. He considered that the alternative manufacturer who had quoted a higher price would be in a better position to meet the delivery requirement. The sales manager of this second company was called in to discuss the matter further and he was able to convince the Production Manager of Company *A* that the promised delivery date would be met; but to secure the order he had to agree to a penalty clause for late delivery.

In Company *B* there was little difference between the four suppliers asked to quote, either in technical performance or price. Each supplier had offered acceptable delivery dates and it seemed as if each and every one could provide a satisfactory 'package' if asked to go ahead. One company had been particularly active in the early stages in assisting the engineers of Company *B* to solve a design problem, and had also kept its delivery promises made to an associated company purchasing similar equipment. These two 'plusses' were sufficient to distinguish this particular supplier from its competitors. In a situation similar to that in the example of Company *A*, the Buyer of Company *C* chose the supplier offering the better delivery date, once he was satisfied that both possible contenders for the business were acceptable to the development personnel.

In Company *D* the technical preference had narrowed from a possible twenty suppliers to a short list of two. The order was given to the company which had the better 'commercial' reputation. In Company *E*, the supplier evaluation and selection was made on the basis of the technical recommendations and solutions offered by the one supplier contacted.

DMU Members Involved

It is at the stage when quotations are evaluated that the Buyer begins to share the decision on the final selection of supplier. Up to this point he is generally content to leave the negotiations between his company and outside suppliers to the technical personnel involved and he is prepared, in new product purchases, to accept their recommendations, and usually their preferences for one particular supplier who has been helpful at the early problem solving stages.

Some buyers interviewed saw their role in the new purchase situation as simply purchasing, within budget limitations, the items required by the technical staff. If, however, a choice had to be made, for example, between two companies equally acceptable in the technical sense, the Buyer was found to exert a great deal of influence on final selection through his skills of commercial appraisal, on matters such as price, delivery, backing services and ease of commercial communication.

Setting Up Order Routine and Performance Feedback

The order routine varies with the type of goods purchased. The plant equipment examples given obviously did not become repeat items but the roller bearings and edible casings were purchased regularly after the initial orders had been placed. Such product as these become repeat purchases and can best be reviewed as such (pages 61–65). The less frequently purchased items require no order routine but do not escape evaluation.

4

Changing from a Regular
to a New Supplier

see p120 Appendix C

Reasons for change

Industrial purchasing is a process involving a variety of individuals at different time periods in activities of varying intensities. When products new to the Company are required, the activity is concentrated on planning the type of product, the preparation of detailed specifications and the search for possible suppliers. At a later stage in the purchasing process these technical deliberations are combined with the commercial expertise of the professional buyer, a supplier is selected and the purchase is made. Once the decision is made to go ahead with the purchase, the technical personnel involved in the early stages of the purchase move on to help solve another problem which may require a further new purchase for its solution.

At the other end of the purchasing spectrum, quantities of repeat purchases are made without reference to technical or non-technical decision makers. At some earlier time these repeat purchases would have been new purchases but now the emphasis has shifted away from the detailed discussion of what to buy from which supplier to the more straightforward, but no less vital task, of getting the product in at regular intervals to satisfy the needs of the using departments.

From time to time, however, events occur disturbing the routine pattern of a repeat purchase which may ultimately lead to a change from a regular to a new supplier, but the following cases are representative of the change situations. The examples show a change in supplier resulting from:

- irritation caused by a change in the commercial procedures of a supplier

- creative marketing by a potential supplier
- increase in price by an existing supplier
- poor delivery by an existing supplier.

Other reasons include those prompted by the changing needs of customers such as complaints regarding the timing sequence of an electronic timer fitted as a key component in machinery supplied by an original equipment manufacturer, or a change in electric motor suppliers to meet the needs of a customer requiring tropicalised vending machines. These were studied first as modifications of repeat purchase patterns, but the purchasing modifications resulting from changed technical requirements were being treated by the respondent companies as new purchases. The alternative or substitute product eventually purchased was not identical to the one originally employed.

Changing Supplier Case Examples

Company A: Food Processing:
Change in Commercial Procedures of Supplier

RECOGNITION OF
NEED TO
PURCHASE

Company *A* made large regular purchases of kraft string for sewing bags from a preferred supplier until that company introduced a new method of despatch by boxing the spools in dozens. Previously the spools had arrived unboxed but now a surcharge of 12½p was to be made for the box which was unreturnable.

The BUYER at Company *A* objected to the surcharge and to the trouble of having to dispose of the unwanted boxes. Formal complaint was made on three separate occasions and a change in supplier threatened. Meanwhile the surcharge went unpaid. The kraft supplier, however, refused to alter his conditions of delivery pointing out that the boxing of spools had become accepted throughout the industry.

DESCRIPTION OF
PRODUCT
CHARACTERISTICS

The kraft was sold to a certain standard. There was no need to reassess the product of an alternative supplier if the same standard could be obtained.

SEARCH FOR
POTENTIAL
SUPPLIERS

When he realised that the existing supplier would not budge on terms the BUYER began an active search for an alternative supplier. Eventually he found a manufacturer of kraft to the same quality who would agree to deliver without the box surcharge.

SELECTION OF
SUPPLIER

The BUYER switched his company's regular order for kraft to the new supplier after assuring himself that an identical quality could be obtained and that continuity of supply could be guaranteed.

FEEDBACK AND
SUPPLIER
EVALUATION

The original kraft supplier dropped the box surcharge in an effort to regain the business lost but the user department had made no complaints about the change to the new supplier and the Buyer would not consider any new move unless a reduction in price of 10 per cent were offered. The original supplier was not able to make this reduction.

Company B: Paper Industry:
Creative Marketing by Supplier

RECOGNITION OF
NEED TO
PURCHASE

Company *B* was dependent on one British manufacturer for the continued supply of an important chemical used in a coating process. SALES REPRESENTATIVES of a West German company visited the BUYER of Company *B* and offered the equivalent chemical at a higher price but processed in such a way that a considerable reduction would be obtained in (Company *B*'s) manufacturing costs.

DESCRIPTION
OF PRODUCT
CHARACTERISTICS

The BUYER, keen to reduce his dependence on a single source of supply encouraged the West German company to provide more technical details for presentation to the technical personnel who would need to be convinced of the merits of any change.

SEARCH FOR
POTENTIAL
SUPPLIERS

While awaiting further details from the West German firm, the BUYER located a French supplier. He also advised the existing British manufacturer of his negotiations with alternative suppliers.

QUALIFICATIONS
OF POTENTIAL
SUPPLIERS

The PRODUCTION personnel responsible for the quality of Company *B*'s product were very reluctant to accept any change in materials used in what they regarded as a highly satisfactory manufacturing process. The BUYER persevered in his support for the foreign product and technical evidence provided by a chemist visiting from the West German company was finally accepted by the TECHNICAL decision makers.

EVALUATION OF
PROPOSALS

After some deliberation, the British supplier agreed to offer the chemical similarly processed and at a price lower than the West German quotation. The French price was also lower than the West German but the BUYER considered that the French manufacturing facility was not yet sufficient to meet the regular requirement of Company *B*. There was also some doubt regarding the quantities available from the West German Plant.

SELECTION OF
SUPPLIER

The new offer made by the British supplier was accepted.

SELECTION OF
ORDER ROUTINE

A fixed price contract was signed renewable in one year. Both supplier and purchaser were reluctant to commit themselves further than one year.

PERFORMANCE
FEEDBACK AND
SUPPLIER
EVALUATION

The performance of the British supplier was acceptable on both technical and commercial grounds. Reports were being obtained, however, on the availability and condition of supply of the chemical from the alternative foreign sources.

Company C: Heating and Ventilating Contracting: Creative Marketing by Potential Supplier

RECOGNITION
OF NEED TO
PURCHASE

Company C purchased regular supplies of copper tubing from a manufacturer selling through a nominated distributor. Representatives of competitor manufacturers had called at frequent intervals but had been unable to secure any of Company C's copper tubing business as their prices were not sufficiently competitive to warrant the disturbance involved in a change of supplier.

One competitor SALES REPRESENTATIVE, however, arrived one day with the offer of copper tubing supplied direct from the manufacturer at prices 10 per cent lower than those of the nominated distributor currently used.

DESCRIPTION
OF PRODUCT
CHARACTERISTICS

The copper tubing used was manufactured to a British standard.

QUALIFICATIONS
OF POTENTIAL
SUPPLIER

The BUYER wanted to take advantage of the reduced price but Company C had had no previous dealings with this direct supplier. Before making a decision he telephoned a number of other Buyers in the same industry asking if they had purchased copper tubing direct from the supplier concerned. He was particularly interested in such factors as delivery, standard terms of payment and the opportunities for direct contact with company personnel other than the sales representative.

SELECTION OF
SUPPLIER AND
ORDER ROUTINE

The BUYER at Company *C* obtained favourable answers to the questions put to his purchasing colleagues and he decided to go ahead switching one seventh of his current order for copper tubing to the new direct supplier.

PERFORMANCE
FEEDBACK AND
EVALUATION

Particular attention was paid to the quality of the tubing and the new supplier's ability to meet promised delivery dates. The BUYER was planning to increase the proportion of orders placed with the new company.

Company D: Electrical Industry:
Reaction to Price Increase

RECOGNITION
OF NEED TO
PURCHASE

For two years Company *D* had regularly purchased printed circuit boards to an agreed specification and design from one well known supplier. Relations between the two companies had been good particularly on the technical side as the printed boards were of high quality and the staff responsible for checking the quality of components used in production had voiced no complaints.

The suppliers' high reputation had been questioned, however, by PRODUCTION and STOCK CONTROL when promised delivery dates had not been met. This disrupted the lead time calculations and on one occasion had nearly led to a costly hold up in production. These were spasmodic events, however, and no move had been made to change to another supplier. The problem arose when the supplier announced, in a postal circular, a 20 per cent increase in the price of the printed boards regularly purchased by Company *D*. A price increase of this size was sufficient to evoke an immediate reaction and the BUYER, prompted in the main by the cost factor but reinforced by the memory of the embarrassingly low stock levels, decided to seek an alternative source of supply.

DESCRIPTION
OF PRODUCT
CHARACTERISTICS

The BUYER informed the DESIGN engineers of the price increase and of his intention to change suppliers if possible. The DESIGN engineers reported back that no change in the technical specification of the printed board in question was contemplated. They would wish to approve any new supplier.

SEARCH FOR
POTENTIAL
SUPPLIERS

The search for an alternative supplier was a simple straightforward operation. The SALES REPRESENTATIVE of a competitor supplier had called on a number of occasions during the previous twelve months and details of his company's products were on file. The representative was called in and invited to quote for the supply of printed circuit boards identical to those in use.

QUALIFICATIONS
OF POTENTIAL
SUPPLIER

Sample circuits were supplied and tested and passed by the DESIGN engineers of Company *D*.

ACQUISITION OF
PROPOSALS

The price offered was marginally higher than the existing suppliers' price before the 20 per cent increase.

EVALUATION
OF PROPOSALS

Once the new printed circuit boards had received technical approval, the BUYER went ahead with the details of the commercial negotiation before placing an order.

During these negotiations the BUYER was unpleasantly surprised to learn, for the first time, of a special tooling cost which the new supplier wished to charge to cover the additional cost of drilling the fixing holes on the board. On enquiry, the BUYER learned that if these holes could be moved to a standard position, no special tooling cost would be charged.

The BUYER promptly referred the problem to the DESIGN engineers who agreed that there was sufficient room in the equipment being manufactured for the board to be fixed by the standard holes suggested.

SELECTION OF
SUPPLIER/
SELECTION OF
ORDER ROUTINE

After calculating the phasing of deliveries and ensuring continuity of supply, the BUYER placed his regular order for printed circuit boards with the new supplier and cancelled future orders that had been lodged with the existing supplier.

Company E: Engineering:
Poor Delivery by Existing Supplier

RECOGNITION
OF NEED TO
PURCHASE

The BUYER in Company *E* initiated the change in the supply of gaskets owing to the continued poor delivery performance of the existing supplier.

DESCRIPTION
OF PRODUCT
CHARACTERISTICS

The ENGINEERING department was informed of the possibility of a change in supplier but no detailed discussion was necessary as there was to be no alteration to the specification already agreed.

SEARCH FOR POTENTIAL SUPPLIER/ ASSESSING QUALIFICATIONS	Three alternative suppliers, all well-known to the BUYER through previous contact, were approached.
ACQUISITION OF PROPOSALS	SALES REPRESENTATIVES of all three companies called on the BUYER and quotations for equivalent gaskets obtained.
SELECTION OF SUPPLIER	Each of the three potential suppliers had good commercial and technical reputations. The BUYER selected the company offering the lowest price.
SELECTION OF ORDER ROUTINE	The regular order for gaskets was switched to the new supplier and the STOCK CONTROLLER informed of the change.
PERFORMANCE FEEDBACK AND EVALUATION	A 'value analysis' committee evaluates all repeat purchases once a year.

Changing from a
Regular to a New Supplier:
Stages of the Purchasing Process

In contrast to the procedures for buying products new to the company during which a number of different members of the DMU interact through various stages of decision taking, the process by which regular orders are re-directed from an established to a new supplier is dominated throughout by only one member of the DMU, namely the Buyer.

Recognition of the Need to Purchase

The stimulus for the change in each case comes from outside the company but unlike the external stimuli which led to the new product purchases, the first point of impact is not the Board or General Manager but the Buyer.

In the Company *A* example the Buyer was able to react to what he regarded as a high-handed commercial practice without any prompting from other DMU members. Similarly, in Companies *D* and *E*, where a sudden price rise and continued poor delivery performance were sufficient in themselves to activate the Buyer and thereby lead to a change.

The Buyers of Companies *B* and *C* are shown reacting to a more welcome external stimulus, that of a constructive, profit benefit suggestion by a manufacturers' sales representative. Although in one case the increased profitability was offered through a technical change and in the other a simple price reduction, the first point of contact for the outsider was the Buyer. Interest was created on both occasions and the purchasing process was allowed to proceed.

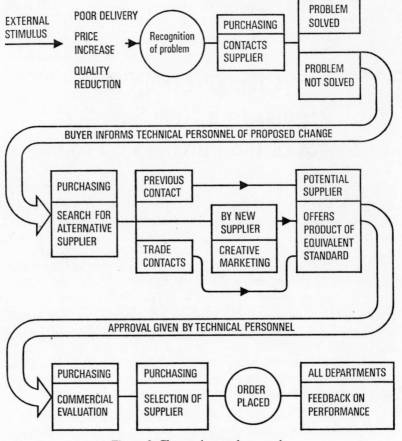

Figure 3 Change in regular supply

Description of Product Characteristics

Where a change in supplier rather than a change in technical requirement is contemplated, the Buyer concerned does little more than keep the technical personnel involved informed as to what he is about to do.

The Buyer in Company *B*, however, had a more complicated task before him. Although keen to make considerable savings in the process cost of the chemical used he realised that no progress could be made without the wholehearted support of the Production men who took a pride in the company's reputation for quality. If 'cheaper' was to mean 'nastier' then the deal was off. Hence the Buyer supported the efforts made by the West German manufacturer to convince his technical colleagues of the merits of the change and more important, that the quality of the end product would not be a risk.

The Buyer at Company *D* also expended a great deal of effort in order to keep open the channels of communication between the technical personnel of the printed circuit company and his own company's design engineers regarding the positioning of the fixing holes on the board.

Search for Potential Suppliers

Where new suppliers are required the Buyer is the main initiator of the search, but as the companies chosen are already likely to be well known, the search does not need to be very extensive. Those alternative or competitor suppliers who have maintained contact are most likely to be called in. In Company *A* the Buyer had the more protracted task of not only locating a supplier of kraft, but also one who would be prepared to defer the 'trade custom' of charging for spool boxes, before any serious negotiations could continue.

In the Company *B* example, the Buyer could have restricted his negotiations to the West German supplier who initiated the possibility of change, but instead he sought out a French manufacturer also prepared to supply the processed chemical required. The main benefit of the change would have been financial but the Buyer at Company *B*, although keen to obtain this financial advantage, was also concerned with securing a regular supply.

Qualifications of Potential Suppliers

None of the new suppliers considered lacked technical credibility but naturally enough, the change from one to another or the diversification of sources of supply could not proceed without the approval of the purchasing company's technical personnel. Where products such as copper tubing or motor gaskets were purchased to an agreed British or International Standard, the approval procedure was relatively straight forward involving little more than the courtesy of one DMU member, the Buyer, keeping other DMU members—design engineers or stock controllers—informed of what he was doing and why he was doing it.

In the printed circuit board example, considerable liaison between Buyer and Design Engineer was necessary during the purchasing process but there was no resistance to the change from the technical personnel once they had been able to test sample circuit boards sent in by the new supplier.

In Company *B* the chemical to be supplied passed the necessary laboratory tests but as it was to be used outside laboratory conditions in a manufacturing process, production personnel had also to be convinced of the West German manufacturer's ability to provide a product of continuing quality. It is clear, therefore, that although a non-technical DMU member, the Buyer had been responsible (on occasion aided by the promotional efforts of an outsider) for the early stages of the process of change, any potentially new supplier had to prove himself capable of manufacturing to the required technical specification before any further action could be taken.

When possible, the Buyer and a production equipment or design engineer will visit the premises of any contending supplier to satisfy themselves as to the company's technical and manufacturing facilities, but the examples obtained of such an event taking place were associated more with new purchases than with a change of suppliers. With or without a visit, however, once technical approval has been obtained, the Buyer needs to assess the commercial qualifications of a new supplier. In Companies *D* and *E* regular contact by representatives of potential suppliers and the reputation of their companies, had satisfied the Buyer on points of commercial acceptability. In Company *C*, the Buyer contacted other Buyers to discover more directly the new suppliers reputation.

Selection of Supplier

In the examples, Companies *A*, *B*, *C* and *D*, the underlying reason for the proposals to change suppliers was a cost benefit. Once the technical details had been settled and continuity of supply assured, the selection of supplier was made on the basis of the contribution to cost saving.

5

Routine Re-purchases

New purchases and the change from regular to new suppliers discussed in the previous two chapters are typified by bursts of intense activity of relatively limited duration. The shared decision making which surrounds the purchase of products new to the company finally comes to an end, however, with the placing of an order and the satisfactory installation of some new piece of equipment or use of a new component or material. If the product is required regularly for production or for non-manufacturing supplies, an order routine is established and a repeat purchase cycle begins. Similarly when problems which lead to a change in suppliers are eventually solved regular purchases recommence.

In contrast to the varying patterns of the first-time or modified purchase, the routine of the repeat purchase described below offers less spectacular but nonetheless important implications for the approved supplier wishing to hold on to regular orders and for the potential supplier keen to break into new business.

Company A: Engineering Industry:
Repeat Purchase of Small Fasteners

RECOGNITION OF NEED TO PURCHASE	The purchase was triggered off by a STOCK CONTROL SYSTEM which indicated when further orders had to be placed in order to maintain an agreed minimum stock level.
DESCRIPTION OF PRODUCT CHARACTERISTICS	A detailed description of the fasteners to be purchased was contained on the stock control record card.

SEARCH FOR
POTENTIAL
SUPPLIERS

No search for suppliers was made. The names of four approved suppliers were listed in the re-order instructions.

QUALIFICATIONS
AND SELECTION
OF SUPPLIERS

The latest price lists, discount terms and delivery lead times for each of the four approved suppliers were received by an ASSISTANT BUYER. The supplier offering the most favourable terms was selected.

If all four companies offer similar prices and delivery dates, the Assistant Buyer would telephone their respective sales offices to verify the accuracy of the information. In this particular case, however the Assistant Buyer was prepared to accept the details left with him by the SALES REPRESENTATIVE of one of the four companies who had recently called, without any further reference to the other three suppliers listed.

Company B: Vehicle Industry:
Repeat Purchase of High Duty Alloy

RECOGNITION
OF NEED TO
PURCHASE

A computer, programmed to retain estimates of average use of high duty alloys over a period of six months, was fed details of existing stock and current actual usage. The computer calculated the amount to be purchased to maintain stock levels.

DESCRIPTION
OF PRODUCT
CHARACTERISTICS

The agreed specification for repeat orders was held in the BUYING Department.

SEARCH FOR
POTENTIAL
SUPPLIERS

At the request of the Ministry involved in the overall cost control of the projects for which alloys were required, a minimum of three alternative suppliers were listed in the repeat order instructions.

ASSESSING
QUALIFICATIONS
AND SELECTING
SUPPLIER

A specialist BUYER contacted all three suppliers for delivery dates and latest prices. A purchase requisition was raised in favour of the supplier with the lowest price.

Company C: Metal Industry:
Repeat Purchase of Bearings

RECOGNITION
OF NEED TO
PURCHASE

Withdrawals of bearings by the user department were noted on card in a 'maximum-minimum' stock control system and the re-order point reached.

DESCRIPTION
OF PRODUCT
CHARACTERISTICS
SEARCH FOR
SUPPLIERS

The card gave stock code, user department, names of four suppliers and full description and specification. The STOCK CONTROLLER at the re-order point checked the latest information available on delivery and price.

EVALUATING
OF PROPOSALS

The CENTRAL PURCHASING department had made arrangements with the four possible suppliers through which purchasing departments in various regional locations could receive the benefit of a bulk price discount, less 20 per cent, based on the company's total national purchases.

SELECTION
OF SUPPLIER

SALES REPRESENTATIVES of the four preferred suppliers called regularly, leaving details of prices and delivery. This particular re-order was allocated to the supplier with delivery ex stock, but attention was given throughout the year to all four companies so that alternative sources of supply could be maintained.

SELECTION OF
ORDER ROUTINE

The STOCK CONTROLLER was permitted to initiate orders up to £50. He raised a purchase request note which contained the quantities, price and nominated supplier. The order was placed by PURCHASING department staff as a matter of routine.

Routine Re-purchases
Stages of the Purchasing Process

Regular repurchases are delegated by the Buyer to assistant buyers, stock controllers and other clerical staff. Members of the DMU outside the purchasing department are not involved.

Recognition of Need to Purchase

Repurchases are initiated by stock control systems varying in degrees of sophistication from computer control to a simple card routine. A minimum stock level is set and when this is reached the re-ordering process begins.

Description of Product Characteristics

No technical decisions are taken as the specification required are laid down in the re-order instructions.

Search for Potential Suppliers

No search is carried out. The names of preferred suppliers are contained within the re-order instructions.

Evaluating Proposals and Supplier Selection

In the short term members of the Purchasing Department evaluate suppliers on the basis of the most recent information relating to prices, deliveries and lead times but in the longer term continuity of supply is regarded as an important factor. Continuity of supply is normally sought by the nomination of more than one preferred supplier but in those cases where only one supplier was used, it was

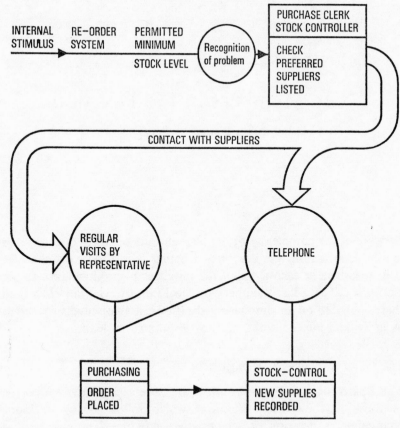

Figure 4 Repeat purchase

found that continuity was obtained by contracting orders for regular deliveries over a period or through very close liaison between supplier and purchaser. One Purchasing Company, submitted its production schedules to one component supplier who scheduled his own production stock-holding in accord with the required rate of deliveries.

Where a number of preferred suppliers offer similar terms, however, selection is likely to be influenced by the effectiveness of the calls made by suppliers' representatives and by personal likes and dislikes.

6

Key Members of the Decision Making Unit

Because of the complexity of the task and the numbers of executives involved, attention was drawn in Chapter 3 to the involvement of DMU members at each stage of the purchase of products new to the Company. These key members of the Decision Making Unit, and their contribution to purchasing decisions, as individuals or rather as individual job functions, are now examined in depth.

The Board and General Management

The Board or general management are necessarily heavily involved in those new purchase situations which follow policy decisions changing the direction of a company's activities. The emphasis at this level is on the longer term decision taken to guide the company so that the maximum return on investment will be obtained from available resources.

Once the policy decision has been made, for example, to diversify into a new market, the detailed preparations for the purchase of the equipment, raw materials or components required to put the decision into effect are delegated. In the new purchase situation general management are responsible for recognising the problem, indirectly starting off the purchasing process from the top downwards by their general solutions to that problem.

New purchases were also located which originated with junior technical personnel and which then proceeded upwards to higher levels of management for approval before a decision to purchase was made. The purchase of the new conveyor equipment started at maintenance engineer level but the purchase order eventually required the endorsement or approval of general management. In both situations whether the procedures emanate from the top and move in a downward direction or from the lower levels to move upwards, general management are not concerned with the selection of potential suppliers or the technical negotiations which determined the selection of the preferred supplier.

Because examples showing Board involvement in supplier selection in the new purchase situation are not reported here it does not follow that such events do not occur. A high cost equipment purchase will return to the Board or general management for final approval at the end of the buying process at the pre-order stage. If the final decision is to be made between one or two technically acceptable suppliers, or if some arbitration is required to smooth out differences of opinion as to the preferred supplier, the Board may well exercise its ultimate power of supplier selection devoid of any marketing influence.

It is the job of the supplier's marketing personnel to convince the companies' technical and commercial decision makers that there is no valid choice between contestants for the order *before* the formal Board approval stage is reached.

Technical Personnel

Technical personnel have the most influence on a first time purchase but it is evident from the many situations studied that, at the early stages, they themselves can be highly influenced by sources of technical information external to the company. The plant equipment engineers responsible for increasing production capacity or the design engineers asked to improve the performance of next year's model have a very clear idea of what is wanted and how, in general terms, it should be brought about, but they frequently lack the detailed knowledge required to put their plans or designs into a form suitable for purchasing decisions to be made. They are 'hungry for information'.

In some cases the technical personnel know where to obtain assistance, in others they have first to seek out possible suppliers before they can proceed with formulating their recommendations. Advice and information is sometimes sought from colleagues in associated companies or non-commercial sources. Suppliers, once located, will be asked to send technical sales representatives and requests are made to visit the factories of potential suppliers to gain more information and the assurance that the manufacturing capability promised by the sales representatives does in fact exist. Obviously the level of demand for information varies according to the sophistication of the product in question and the degree to which potential suppliers are known from any previous contact, but it is clear that key technical personnel involved in the important early stages of a new purchasing decision also have sufficient influence over the final stages to ensure that the supplier who gives them the most assistance with their problem solving is rewarded with the ultimate order, even though his price may be higher at the quotation stage than competitors who have been asked to bid. Unless some exceptional commercial conditions prevent it, the professional buyer will be ready to endorse this desire for good working relations with suppliers who have invested in technical support services and price quotations received from competitive suppliers are reviewed in the knowledge of the advice made available by them at the problem solving stage.

In the purchasing situation where the existing supplier is being changed for another, technical personnel are used in the 'long stop' position by the Buyer, who although anxious to bring about the change for commercial reasons, nevertheless cannot succeed without the approval of those responsible for the original specifications.

Technical personnel may also suggest a change in supplier to permit a design improvement, but the extent of re-design may classify such a change as a 'new' rather than a 'modified' purchase. Technical personnel play no part in the repeat purchase although they are needed to endorse any unfavourable technical evaluation at the feed-back stage.

Supplier Marketing Personnel

The view that 'industrial goods are bought and not sold' is largely true when new purchases are considered, but, like all generalisations, it requires further examination if any message or benefit is to be derived.

Supplier's marketing personnel are rarely present in the preliminary stages of problem recognition but once called in by the purchasing company in a new purchase decision the supplier's marketing personnel become very active. It is clear that the quality of the work of the supplier's marketing and other personnel at the relatively early stages of problem solving determines the likelihood of selection at the final stages of the purchasing process. Commercial hurdles will be met by the sales representative at the later stages but the chances of overcoming these are considerably increased if he can 'get in' to the original problem at an early stage and begin to influence the purchasing situation as soon as possible when meeting urgent requests for technical information.

The most difficult task for the sales representative is to break in an established order routine and to supplant the existing supplier. Here, supplier representation is likely to be called in by the Buyer to help him solve some emergency. Instances of creative marketing where a new supplier representative had convinced the Buyer of the merits of change were located in the research work but rarely. The regular calling for the 'out' supplier is necessary, however, if he is to be invited to bid for any change in supply.

Representatives were found to be most frequently present once the product in question had become a repeat purchase with more than one preferred supplier on the re-order instructions.

The Buyer

Apart from some assistance in the search for new suppliers, buyers or their departments are not involved in the early stages of new purchase decisions. The reason for this is that it is generally accepted that the technical problems associated with new purchases must be solved before detailed commercial considerations of a purchase can be made.

Extreme examples of this view can be found in those companies where the purchasing department simply performs the order function without influencing the decision to purchase in any way, but a more representative picture of the new purchase process is given in *Figure 5* which shows that once the early pre-occupation with technical matters is over, the decision process is shared with the buyer. If the product or service being purchased is unique and general management approval obtained, then the involvement of the purchasing department reverts to the simple conventional model of 'getting on with the paper work'. If, however, more than one potential supplier is approved on technical grounds by the engineering, design or maintenance members of the DMU, then the buyer's influence on the eventual outcome is considerable.

Recognition is given to the need to compensate the potential supplier who has increased his costs by early technical support, but if the technical DMU personnel are not concerned in this way, a buyer can make a recommendation based on commercial factors such as

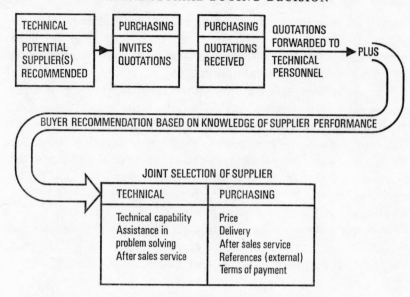

Figure 5 Role of Buyer in new product purchasing

delivery, price, or reputation for ease of communication, which would decide which supplier gets the order. Even where some technical differentiation is present in the competitive products on offer, a buyer with high status, can hold up the order to a recommended supplier until technical justification is offered, to explain the preference for the more expensive or less easily obtainable purchase.

Purchasing personnel are very conscious of the need to keep good relations with the company's technical decision makers, particularly as the increased influence, for example, of standardisation in components or centralised buying introduced to make purchasing economies inevitably reduces the scope (or taxes the ingenuity) of designers working in individual departments. Examples were found during the research of purchasing staff located in design departments in order to ease communications and to introduce the 'purchasing approach' into the early stages of new designs. Well established Buyers, who have gained the confidence of their design or technical colleagues, can contribute far more than a list of names if represented in meetings during which the original problem is being discussed.

Senior engineers largely recognised the role of purchasing as final arbiters where commercial factors were important, but some junior engineers interviewed, particularly on the design side, were not fully aware of their relationship with purchasing. One dispute noted, where the buyer considered over-specification was taking place was soon settled by the chief engineer who supported the buyers recommendations and ordered a change in the design specification in favour of less expensive components.

TABLE 5

DMU MEMBERS INVOLVED BY TYPE OF PURCHASE

Purchasing Stages	New Purchase	Change in Supplier	Repeat Purchase
Recognition of Need to Purchase	Board, General Management	Buyer	Stock Control System
Determination of Product Characteristics	Technical Personnel	As specified when new purchase	As specified
Description of Product Characteristics	Technical Personnel	As specified	As specified
Search for Suppliers	Technical Personnel	Buyer	Approved suppliers
Assessing Qualifications of Suppliers	Technical Personnel	Technical Personnel and Buyer	Approved suppliers
Acquisition of Proposals	Buyer and Technical Personnel	Buyer	Purchasing Staff
Evaluation of Proposals	Technical Personnel	Buyer	Purchasing Staff
Selection of Supplier	Technical Personnel General Management, Buyer	Buyer	Purchasing Staff
Selection of Order Routine	Buyer	Buyer	Purchasing Staff
Performance Feedback and Evaluation	Technical Personnel and Buyer (informal)	Buyer (informal) System (formal)	Buyer (informal) System (formal)

In the modified rebuy purchase where one supplier is being changed for another, the Buyer becomes the leading member of the Decision Making Unit, both as initiator of the change and as the final arbiter of the purchase decision.

Earlier research has claimed the Buyer to be the key decision taker in the repeat purchase situation. It is true that the Buyer has great influence on which companies should become preferred regular suppliers when no technical differentiation is present, but when the repeat orders are actually placed the decision as to which of the listed suppliers gets the order is likely to be made by a junior buyer or clerk in the Purchasing department rather than the Buyer himself.

Accountant and Financial Controller

Financial personnel contribute an 'influencing' factor to the industrial purchasing process as the vast majority of purchases are made within the umbrella of previously agreed budgets.

The repeat purchase of raw materials, for example, may be executed by computer but the amounts to be purchased at different intervals will have been agreed with the financial personnel although they will not have entered into the discussions of specification or even supplier selection unless some reciprocal trading with strong financial implications is involved.

The purchase of capital equipment will similarly require financial or budgetary approval but without participation in the details of the purchasing decision process.

7

What do we know about
Buyer Behaviour?

New entrants to industrial marketing benefit from both their current experiences and also from the advice given by those who supervise their efforts even though the sad truth of the saying that 'wisdom cannot be told' limits the effectiveness of the latter form of learning.

An additional source of information for the new recruit is the growing body of knowledge which has developed from research into various aspects of industrial purchasing behaviour. These inquiries, conducted at spasmodic intervals, have produced results which are highly relevant but so far, little attempt has been made to collect this information together and relate it to the day-to-day activities of the practitioner.

In the hope that, if studied, they will reduce the number of scars earned in the market place, the results of previous research into industrial purchasing practices are examined (with the exception of the *How British Industry Buys* and the Robinson and Faris survey detailed on pages 13–21) and conclusions drawn on their contribution to marketing activities.

IS THE INDUSTRIAL BUYER RATIONAL OR IRRATIONAL?

Relevance of the Research

A large number of approaches can be used in selling and numerous different appeals in advertising. Should these approaches and appeals tend towards the factual or emotional?

The traditional view of the industrial buyer is that of a cool-headed businessman taking rational decisions based on hard facts in order to improve the profitability of his company. In contrast to this picture of rationality can be presented the actions of possibly the same man, or at least his wife, as a member of the consuming public open to impulse purchase and swayed by the emotional appeal of advertising. Doubts have been expressed as to the accuracy of this neat and tidy distinction between industrial and consumer rupchasing, not only on the industrial side but also in the world of the private consumer supported by 'Best Buy' reports and the recommendations of local consumer protection associations.

Before attempting to draw conclusions, however, a hearing should be given to both sides of the question as seen by researchers into industrial buying practices.

Yes—He's Rational

A typical early view was that presented in 1924 by Dr. Copeland, a Professor of Marketing at the Harvard Graduate Business School, when he stated in a chapter entitled 'Buying Motives for Industrial Goods'[1] that 'a reliance on rational motives is logical, as an industrial firm makes its purchases for business reasons and not for the personal gratification of individual executives'. Copeland examined 756 different industrial advertisements in a large number of trade journals and was able to classify the variety of appeals made to those directed to either

BUYING MOTIVES relating to the decision to buy a specific product or commodity, or

PATRONAGE MOTIVES i.e. those motives involved in the selection of a specific supplier.

The range of the two types of appeal are listed in Table 6.

The Buying motives can clearly be claimed to be rational and the classification 'Patronage', although to modern ears implying some irrationality or at least the use of personal rather than impersonal values and judgement, was also intended by Copeland to support his rational view of industrial purchasing. Indeed, a purchasing officer or buyer who selects a regular supplier, whom he knows to be financially stable and punctual on delivery in preference to a cheaper but unknown new supplier, could be seen to be acting rationally.

Copeland's views on rational industrial buying, given some

[1] Copeland, M. T., *Principles of Merchandising*, A. W. Shaw Co., Chicago 1924.

TABLE 6

COPELAND'S REVIEW OF INDUSTRIAL PURCHASING MOTIVES

Buying Motives	Patronage Motives
Economical in use	Reliability of supplier
Improved plant productivity	Punctuality in delivery
Flexible	Exact fulfilment of
Durable	specification requested
Safe-guarding employee welfare	Variety of selection
	Dependability of repair service

50 years ago, still find support in more recent writers on the topic. Tofte[2] has firmly claimed that the industrial buyer is a very rational being who checks the facts relating to a buying recommendation because his job may well depend upon the infallibility of that recommendation. The buyer 'is sticking his neck right out when buying the unknown or unapproved'. Even here, however, in such a forthright claim by a writer who clearly wants to dispel from the reader's mind the suspicion that the industrial buyer could be influenced by irrational motives, there exists the possibility that by keeping his neck 'well in' for the sake of job security he may well take an irrational decision from the company's point of view when dealing with competitor suppliers. It is evident in the statements of these two quite different contributors, that attempts to interpret what is rational or irrational without reference to the environment within which any particular decision is taken are likely to be misleading.

Purchasing as a Two-Way Process

A more considered view, which in the main supports the rational element in industrial buying, is that which recognises the increasing status of the industrial purchasing function as a profit making centre in its own right. This implies the abandonment of the passive role of purchasing, that is, the simple ordering up of what is required, and its replacement by the more active role of seeking out new sources of supply and of weighing up alternative courses of action, possibly independent of the appeals and recommendations of marketers

[2] Tofte, A. R., 'They Don't Buy Bulldozers the Way They Buy Beer', *Industrial Marketing*, March 1960.

hoping to supply them. This has led to the remark that 'industrial goods are bought and not sold'.

Clohesey[3] refers to this positive activity as procurement sophistication which is profit orientated, management minded and professional. He points to the impact of technology on the dynamics of buying, the computer, automated paperwork and the realisation by modern management that the purchasing function is related to design, engineering, quality control and production scheduling. Using a machine based concept, EPQ (Economic Purchasing Quantity) a buyer may give a contract not for the lowest price, but to the supplier who can cut the customers inventory cost. Here a possible irrational act of ignoring a low price becomes a highly rational one when supported by this type of sophisticated analysis.

Supplier Evaluation

F. A. Johne[4] refers to surveys conducted by the American *Purchasing Magazine* which indicate an increasing use by purchasing managers of formal systems of supplier evaluation, the majority based on a weighted point system. In varying degrees of sophistication, companies attempt to evaluate their suppliers' technical and engineering efficiency, their production facility and capacity, their financial resources or credit rating and managerial ability as demonstrated through the administrative procedures associated with customer relationships.

Johne goes on to describe a simple weighted point system suggested by the American National Association of Purchasing Agents which assesses purchased goods according to cost, quality and service criteria translated to a weighted scale and recorded as opposite.

The quality ratings show the proportion of lots received and passed by Quality Control; the price rating shows the relationship between net delivered price, including discounts and delivery charges, to the lowest net delivered price; and the service rating the more subjective assessment of the proportion of promises kept by suppliers.

More complicated systems, involving detailed cost ratios are available and have been implemented by the more advanced companies on both sides of the Atlantic. The majority of British companies

[3] Clohesey, J. E., 'The Polished Purchasers', *Sales Management*, August 7, 1964.

[4] Johne, F. A., 'Supplier Evaluation Schemes within the Context of the Industrial Marketing Transaction, *Marketing Forum*, January–February 1970, Institute of Marketing.

	Supplier A			Supplier B			Supplier C		
	'67	'68	'69	'67	'68	'69	'67	'68	'69
Quality Ratio (40 points max.)									
Price Ratio (35 points max.)									
Service Rating (25 points max.)									
Composit Rating (1100 points max.)									

however, although aware of supplier deficiencies through the close attention given by professional Buyers to such details, have yet to introduce formal systems of supplier evaluation.

The cost of implementing such schemes of supplier evaluation, or indeed of searching for sources of supply, has delayed their wider acceptance. Even Buyers, who appear to be efficient in other respects query whether the cost of such information in time and money is worth the result.

It is clear to anyone acquainted with the Stock Market that businessmen *in general* do not know how to maximise profits and one important reason for this is that they lack the information processing systems which contribute to profit maximisation. The managements of such companies are operating a 'satisficing' policy which does not encourage experimentation or risk once profit levels have reached a minimum acceptable point.

Pressures on profit ratios are changing the view of what is acceptable, however, and a growing body of British literature both in the form of text books and articles in professional journals[5] draws attention to the increasing sophistication of industrial purchasing procedures.

Materials Management

A logical extension of these developments is the creation of the new management function of materials management (*Figure 6*), beginning with the selection of suppliers and continuing right through until the

[5] Compton, H. K., 'Supplies and Materials Management', *Business Books*, London 1968. Also Bibliography page.

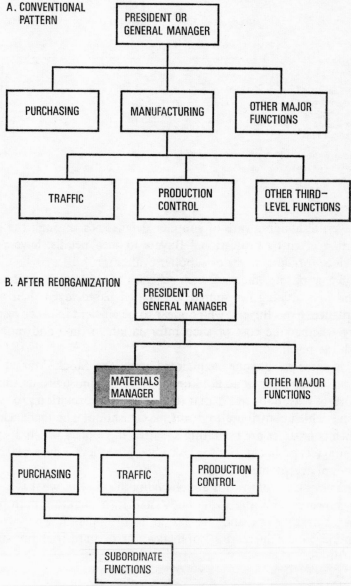

Figure 6 Transition to a materials management organisation
(*Source: D. Ammer, 'Materials Management as a Profit Center'. 'Harvard Business Review':*
January–February, 1969)

purchased material is delivered to its point of use. Dean Ammer[6]
refers to this as responsibility for, 'adding value by distribution to
purchases of direct material (i.e. material used *in* the product) up to

[6] Ammer, D. S., 'Materials Management as a Profit Center', *Harvard Business
Review*, January–February 1969.

the point where manufacturing converts it into a product and thereby adds value by manufacture; with indirect materials (i.e. those used in making the product but not incorporated in it), the Materials Manager performs essentially the same function as a captive industrial distributor. He buys supplies and stores them until they are, in effect, repurchased by their ultimate users.

For convenience, the materials manager may also provide warehousing, traffic, scheduling, trucking and other services for both manufacturing and marketing'.

This increasing status of the purchasing function and its wider control over activities other than buying as such, was noted during the field research in companies where the Head Buyer was in fact involved in the functions described by Ammer and supported by the staff responsible for the contact with the user department and the actual buying from outside suppliers.

No—the Buyer is only Human

Counter to the view of rational behaviour is the claim that the industrial buyer sitting in his office is prone to the same emotions which influence his purchase of retail goods when acting in his capacity as a private consumer. Marino[7] suggests that the industrial buyer is ignorant and needs information. He advises industrial advertisers to use the human approach as '90 per cent of a man's working hours are spent thinking about himself'. A buyer's for example, reacts to the fear of his company becoming outmoded and falling behind its competitors and therefore, advertisers should go ahead and exploit this fear.

A more professional study of the emotive forces in industrial buying is the work carried out by Dr. Shoaf[8] of the University of New York, who took as his hypothesis, 'the industrial buyer makes purchasing decisions on an emotional as well as a rational basis'.

From unstructured interviews with 137 managers randomly selected from 70 companies, Shoaf deduced certain characteristics of industrial buyers, two of which have a direct bearing on his behaviour:

> (a) the industrial buyer is likely to be a conformist—an organisation man. This produces a conflict because although he

[7] Marino, S. F., 'Five Hidden Obstacles to Industrial Selling', *Industrial Marketing*, May 1961.

[8] Shoaf, R. F., 'Here's Proof—The Industrial Buyer Is Human', *Industrial Marketing*, May 1959. Shoaf's findings are also presented in Lazo, H. 'Emotional Aspects of Industrial Buying', *AMA Proceedings*, January 1960.

wants to grow and 'be a hero' in helping his company to grow, he is also security minded and wishes to play safe and impress the boss.

(b) as products and services become more objectively alike, the buyer's final decision is more and more based on subjective emotional factors. — *entertainment*

The great majority of industrial buying decisions, claims Shoaf, are made on an emotional basis. He gives as an example the resistance offered by buyers who fight change for the sake of continuity and the security of dealing with well known suppliers. Shoaf states,

'A buyer enjoys identification with prestige, urged by his insecurity to identify with authority or driven by price to associate with prestige.'

The reaction of the buyer to the late delivery problem is also given as a further example of personal and emotional decision taking. He admits that this may well be a rational consideration (as presumably a costly hold up in production could result) but Shoaf would also, through the buyers' eyes, see late delivery as a suppliers poor attitude to the purchasing company, injurious to the buyer's pride and status and reflecting on his own ability.

The purchasing decisions based in the current research which contained fear of late delivery were found to be more rationally than emotionally based. In the particular example quoted in Chapter 3 (Company *A*, page 31) a delay in the delivery of the mould would have delayed the start of production and the sales targets planned for diodes would have been unobtainable. Delivery was regarded as so important that possible higher technical quality (from the United States) or lower price (from a local but untried supplier) were ignored in favour of the company considered capable of delivering the goods on time. But in addition to the selection of the supplier on these grounds a further rational action was taken by the insistence on the inclusion in the contract with the supplier of a very severe penalty clause for late delivery.

Other delivery decision examples were traced to important and very realistic situations, but it is true that purchases will continue to be made from well known suppliers if no problems have been encountered and there has been no initiative for change. The repeat purchase process described in the research examples shows how the same 'preferred' suppliers can be used to the exclusion of other, possibly cheaper, sources.

An example of the effect of Shoaf's findings on industrial marketing commentators is the interpretation given to them by Sawyer in recommending advertising and promotional appeals. Sawyer claims[9] that industrial marketers should take advantage of the buyers' complacency and inertia and bring transactions more on to the personal level by offering emotional incentives. If the buyer fears decision making:

> 'tell him how clever he is—suggest it will lead to promotion. Constantly assure the buyer in order to feed his appetite for security. Minimise personal difficulties of a switch in supplier in order to pander to his laziness. Play on his craving for status by addressing the buyer as "Manager" '.

This blatant appeal to personal satisfactions is directly comparable to the approaches traditionally used in consumer advertising, but very little notice appears to have been taken by industrial advertisers of this extreme interpretation of Shoaf's views.

Pre-dating Shoaf, a highly regarded study by Duncan[10] led to the conclusion that businessmen are motivated by profit but that in reality the profit motive 'resolves itself into a large number of interelated parts or motives subordinate to this major objective'. While taking the overall view, therefore, that industrial purchasing is rational, Duncan found that many purchases of industrial goods are made on a non-rational basis as a matter of habit.

CONCLUSION   It is clear that industrial purchasing decisions are not solely governed by a rational review of the problem posed if 'rational' is to be interpreted as a long, fully considered view of all possible alternatives in order to obtain maximum company profitability. It is also apparent, however, that actions taken which do not accord with this every-day view of rationality cannot be described as totally irrational or 'emotional'. In theory, for example, a full search for potential suppliers should lead to the opportunity of increasing profitability through purchasing from the cheapest and yet most efficient sources. An examination of actual search procedures used, however, will show that within the time available a quick solution in supplier selection may be more profitable than the results of a thorough, but lengthy, search. — *like serves again.*

The marketing practitioner can steer his way through this paradox

[9] Sawyer, H. G., 'What Does the Industrial Buyer's Emotional Involvement Mean to You?' *Industrial Marketing*, May 1959.
[10] Duncan, D. J., 'What Motivates Business Buyers', *HBR* 1940.

if he is aware that other purchasing motives subordinate to the major objective of profit are present and that these need to be handled in a way which reduces the emphasis on emotion. This can be done by the understanding of purchasing as risk taking.

Purchasing Behaviour as Risk Taking

The concept of purchasing behaviour as risk taking has developed largely from studies of our deliberations and preparations for the purchase of consumer goods. The concept introduced by Raymond Bauer[11] in 1960 is so fundamental, however, that it deserves to be examined not only in its applications to consumer behaviour but also to the current topic of industrial purchasing behaviour. The concept as stated by Bauer is as follows:

> 'Consumer behaviour involves risk in the sense that any action of a consumer will produce consequences which he cannot anticipate with anything approaching certainty,' also that

> 'Consumers characteristically develop decision strategies and ways of reducing risk that enable them to act with relative confidence and ease in situations where their information is inadequate and the consequences of their actions are in some meaningful sense incalculable.'

No consumer would be able to consider the full consequence of the many actions or purchasing decisions he takes and anyone who consistently tried to act like the classical 'rational man' would no doubt become so undecided that he would take no action at all.

To amplify his claim Bauer refers to brand loyalty which could be seen as a means by which the consumer economises his decision effort (and thus reducing risk) by substituting habit for repeated, deliberate, decisions. The popular view that advertising gives 'added value' to a product can also be considered in the light of the risk taking concept. One consumer motive is to have a feeling of confidence in the product he buys and some consumers are prepared to pay a higher price for this added confidence. But not all consumers react in this way. Others would prefer to gain more detailed information from consumer reports in the hopes of finding a less advertised brand rated as 'best buy'.

The numerous instances located in the research of cautious behaviour by buyers holding key positions but without senior

---

[11] Bauer, R. A., 'Consumer Behaviour as Risk Taking', *Proceedings of 43rd Conference of the American Marketing Association*, 1960.

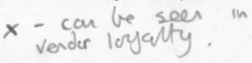

x – can be seen in vendor loyalty.

management status confirm the finding of Monsen and Downs[12] in their investigations into the management of large firms. 'Middle Managers' they claim, 'will normally tend to be risk avoiders in making decisions. A certain degree of advancement can be obtained merely by surviving, doing daily tasks, and not committing any outstanding blunders. . . .' Consequently, the firm may pass up many profit increasing possibilities on the middle management level which would be taken up by the truly profit maximising firm.

Perceived Risk

It should be made clear that 'risk' in the context of consumer behaviour studies refers to perceived risk, or risk as seen by the consumer, even though no risk may exist in reality.

The buyer in an electrical contracting firm (Company C, page 53), who decided to move some of his regular order for copper tubing from his existing supplier to a new supplier offering a lower price, reduced the possibility of any risk in his actions by

- contacting other buyers in the trade to learn of their experiences of the new company.
- switching only $\frac{1}{4}$ of his total order to the new company so that if the new supplier did happen to let him down with deliveries or hidden charges not mentioned by the sales representative, then the purchasing company's contracting operations would not be seriously jeopardised.

Risk Handling in Drug Adoption

The research in risk perception and the methods used by consumers to handle risk has continued since the early 1960's but Bauer himself was responsible for bringing the subject a step nearer to the area of non-domestic behaviour in his studies of doctors and their reaction to the introduction of new drugs by the ethical pharmaceutical companies. Bauer was continuing the work in the medical field of Coleman Katz and Menzel[13] which had confirmed the important role of professional medical sources in reducing the risk of adopting a new drug.

[12] Monsen, R. J. and Downs, A., 'A Theory of the Large Managerial Firm', *Journal of Political Economy*, June 1965.

[13] Coleman, J. F., Katz, E., and Menzel, H. (1957), 'Social Processes in Physicians' Adoption of a New Drug', *Journal of Chronic Diseases*, No. 9, 1959.

It was found that during the early life of a new drug, when insufficient information was available, doctors tended to follow the lead of respected colleagues. Once the drug became sufficiently well established doctors would prescribe it for patients without reference to the personal influence of colleagues.

Bauer found nothing which contradicted these findings but the results of his research showed clearly that doctors also regard the information obtained from well known and trusted pharmaceutical companies and their representatives as highly important. Doctors were found, for example, to minimise risk by prescribing drugs backed by the brand name and reputation of the prominent drug companies in preference to the 'generic' drugs which had similar chemical compositions as the brand drugs but not the backing of known advanced research. This association of risk with company image was to be taken further by Theodore Levitt.[14]

PERCEIVED RISK—CONCLUSIONS   The work carried on by Bauer and others has revealed the importance of understanding why and how customers handle these risks by seeking information and setting up strategies to solve their problems under what they perceive to be varying levels of risk.

THE EFFECTS OF MARKETING COMMUNICATIONS ON INDUSTRIAL PURCHASING BEHAVIOUR

Relevance of the Research

Among the many messages that an industrial sales representatives may take away with him from a sales training course is the advice

First:	Sell your Company
Second:	Sell your Product
As a last resort:	Sell yourself.

The research described below was the first experimental study organised to discover just how important a company's reputation

---

[14] Levitt, T., *Industrial Purchasing Behavior*, Division of Research Graduate School of Business Administration, Harvard University, Boston 1965.

built up by prestige advertising is in relation to the quality of salesman's presentation. Would it pay for example, for a relatively obscure company to spend more money on advertising its name and claimed competence or would the money be better spent on training salesmen to give high quality presentations?

The Research Design

Theodore Levitt, the renowned author of 'Marketing Myopia'[15] devised and administered a highly complex research project at the Harvard Graduate Business School designed to simulate the communication between prospective suppliers of an industrial material and those influencing the purchase of such materials.

Levitt recruited three distinctly different audiences comprising purchasing officers, technical personnel (who are referred in the research report for the sake of brevity as 'chemists') and full-time graduate students of business administration. Each of the three groups of people were split into two separate groups making six groups in all. Levitt's own description of how the research proceeded is reproduced below as although many marketing practitioners may be aware that Levitt has conducted research in the communications area, the details of how he went about collecting the data are less well known. To clarify the picture further, a representation of the research procedure is given in *Figure 7*.

'Each of these audience groups were separately exposed to a single filmed salesman's presentation for a new, technically complex ingredient used in the manufacture of paint. Hence, there were six audience groups—two purchasing agent groups, two chemist groups, and two student groups. There were two different ten minute filmed sales presentations for the same product, a "good" presentation and a "poor" presentation. The stages (or Sets) of both films were identical, as were the actors and the roles they played. One purchasing agent group saw the "good" film and one saw the "poor" film. Similarly one chemist group saw the "good" film and one saw the "poor" one. The same was done with the students.

In addition to dividing each audience category (purchasing agents, technical personnel, and students) into two groups each—one to see the good presentation and one to see the poor presentation—the films

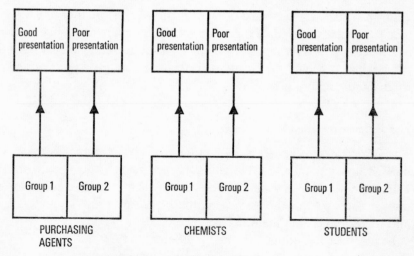

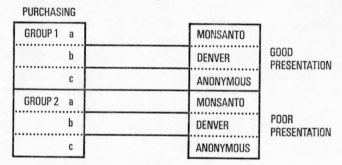

Figure 7 Levitt's Audience Groups

which each of these six groups saw were distinctive for each exposure in one other respect. A third of each of the six groups had its sales- man in the film identified as being from the Monsanto Chemical Company, which in the research is classified as a "high credibility source". Another third of each of the six groups had its salesman in the film identified as being from the Denver Chemical Company, a "medium" credibility source'. And the remaining third of each of the six groups saw a filmed salesman from an anonymous company, a 'low credibility source' for which the name of the company was clearly blocked out.'[16]

[16] Levitt, T., *Industrial Purchasing Behaviour*, Division of Research, Graduate School of Business Administration, Harvard University, Boston, Mass., 1965.

Is a Good Image Important?

An analysis of the research findings confirmed that for complex industrial products or materials a good generalised reputation will favourably influence a company's chances

(1) of getting an attentive first hearing for a new product and

(2) of getting early adoption of that product.

Levitt's original research approach however, enabled him to penetrate far beyond this statement of the general benefits of a good reputation which, with little research backing, has long been the traditional claim of the media space salesman. The variety of sales approaches, by companies of differing reputations to technical and non-technical purchasing influencers produced a number of qualifications to the general statement. One of the most intriguing concerns the impact of a different sales message on the audiences represented in the research.

Company Image and the Technical and Non-Technical Buyer

The research found that the generic group termed 'chemists' who were in fact all graduates currently employed in local industries in some field on engineering or science, were far more influenced by company reputation than the less technically sophisticated professional buyers. This led Levitt to conclude that 'Technical personnel are not human computers whose purchasing and product specification decisions are based on cold calculations and devoid of less rigorously rational influences. They do indeed seem to be influenced by the seller's general reputation.'

Is a Good Sales Presentation Necessary?

If a good company image built up by extensive prestige advertising is so influential then how important is the contributions of an industrial salesman skilled in the art of good presentation? The answer to such a rhetorical question is a positive one but again there are qualifications depending on the risk involved in the purchasing situation, that is the 'risk' as seen by those influencing company purchases. Where the risk was comparatively low (giving a newly presented product a further hearing) the technical personnel were more powerfully influenced by the quality of a direct sales presentation than were the professional buyers.

Where the risk was comparatively high (for example, a decision to buy a new product) the reverse was true. In such a case the technical personnel were found to rely more on their technical judgement of the value of a new product and less on the quality of the sales presentation in favour of that product. The professional buyer, with less technical knowledge to call upon, appeared to rely, in high risk situations more heavily on the seller's presentation.

CONCLUSION   It is safe to assume that a good sales presentation just as a good company reputation, will improve the communication between a supplying company and its prospective customers, but again the combination of reputation ('source effect') and sales effort ('presentation effect') requires closer examination of the impact, particularly of the sales presentation, in different circumstances.

Levitt found that, 'When a relatively unknown or anonymous company makes a good direct sales presentation this combination may be just as effective in getting a favourable first hearing for a complex new industrial material as the combination of a well-known company making a poor presentation.'

A company with a good image still requires sales representatives able to give a skilled presentation if the full benefits of that good image are to be realised. In fact, more skill is expected of the salesman of the well-known company. But, Levitt continues, 'a little-known company, by concentrating strongly on training its salesmen to make good presentations, may be able to make considerable progress toward overcoming the liability of its relative anonymity'. One interpretation of these findings would be that the salesmen of a strong image company maintaining satisfactory service would not have to continue to exert high presentation skills to stay in the business.

Levitt's experimental research has undoubtedly improved our understanding of the effect of sales communications, whether through an image built by advertising or through direct sales presentation.

The examination of actual purchase decisions in the field research has in fact enabled us to amplify the interpretation of 'image' or company reputation. Levitt was limited to the use of 'reputation' as that based on prestige advertising. This was necessary because of the experimental condition of the research but company reputation in the real buying situation is comprised not only on 'prestige image' but also on previous experience of supplier performance, in technical and commercial matters. The professional buyer, and to some extent the engineer, although open to all the influences found by Levitt, also has this other dimension of previous experience or experience of other users by word of mouth advertising, to help them in their decision making.

Degree of Essentiality

In a discussion of the characteristics of industrial goods, Jacqueline Marrian, of the Marketing Department at Lancaster University, introduced the concept of the 'degree of essentiality' which permits a view of industrial purchasing behaviour based on the significance of particular types of commodities to the purpose of the organisation.[17] Some goods essential to company operations, for example, raw materials for production, will receive a great deal of buying attention to ensure regular quality, adequate stock levels, and continuing supply. The purchase of items not considered important, however, could be delayed in time of weakening cash flows or simply treated with less professional attention by a purchasing clerk. The same item may for one firm represent an essential purchase, while for another firm it represents a postponable expenditure.

These variations in the requirements of different customers for the same product or material supplied by one industry account for the variations in buyer behaviour to which industrial marketers must adapt their strategies as potential suppliers. In one prospective customer the quality of the chemical raw material may be so critical that a wide span of technical personnel will be involved in the purchasing decision and once the quality is settled and found satisfactory the Buyer is less likely to take any risks by changing the source of supply. In another customer, the chemical composition of the raw material may not be so critical, enabling the Buyer to seek the best commercial terms he can with little risk of not being able to buy elsewhere if he upsets his existing supplier.

The Status of Industrial Buyers

George Straus[18] has indicated that purchasing agents or professional buyers are sufficiently concerned with their status in an organisation to use any opportunity to influence any purchase decision.

[17] Marrian, J., 'Marketing Characteristics of Industrial Goods and Buyers' in Wilson, A., editor, *The Marketing of Industrial Products*, Pan Books, 1972.

[18] Strauss, G., 'Tactics of Lateral Relationship: The Purchasing Agent', *Admin. Science Quarterly* VII, September 1962.

'The ambitious agent feels that placing orders and expediting deliveries are but the bare bones of his responsibilities. He looks upon his most important function as that of keeping management posted about market developments, new materials, new sources of supply, price trends, and so forth. To make this information more useful, he seeks to be consulted before the requisition is drawn up, while the product is still in the planning stage.'

Support for the conclusions offered by Strauss is given in the results of a survey by James[19] of 24 Scottish firms which showed that in the traditional Scots company the purchasing officer was completely cut off from any vertical or line relationship and that both formal and informal communications were lateral. The purchasing officer enjoyed the 'status' of a staff position but he worked more from specification originating from engineers and other company personnel rather than initiating work himself.

James sees in this situation of relative isolation a natural desire for the purchasing officer to assert himself and in order to boost his position he will resort to many devices including the querying of engineering specifications, demanding more time in which to place an order, querying costs and modifying quantities in the knowledge of inventory levels and price changes.

A further attempt at status building is seen by James in the buyer's efforts to establish active search procedures to collect the most recent information on materials, suppliers and prices. The information received gives the buyer authority.

CONCLUSION It is evident that variations are to be found in the status of the buyer not only between different industries but also within the organisations of different companies in the same industry.

One or two cases were traced in the research where the Buyer in a relatively low status situation, had taken some action such as holding up a small order to combine it with a larger one in the pipeline so that an extra discount could be obtained. This delay in processing the small order caused some irritation in the design department in the company concerned and was interpreted by the engineers interviewed as an attempt by the Buyer to draw attention to the fact that his job was not confined to clerical routine.

In Company *B* (pages 52–53) the Buyer was certainly making himself a focal point of attention in his negotiations with the

19 James, B., 'Emotional Buying in the Industrial Market', *Scientific Business*, Spring 1966.

potentially new West German and French suppliers as he controlled the contacts and the supply of information, but he held a senior position in the company hardly lacking in status. His position of power was also recognised by the British supplier who was persuaded to provide a better service to keep out foreign competition.

In the majority of companies visited, the role of the buyer was seen to be improving not necessarily as a result of his contrived attempts to gain status but because the members of the DMU and senior management generally had recognised the contribution of purchasing to the company's efficiency.

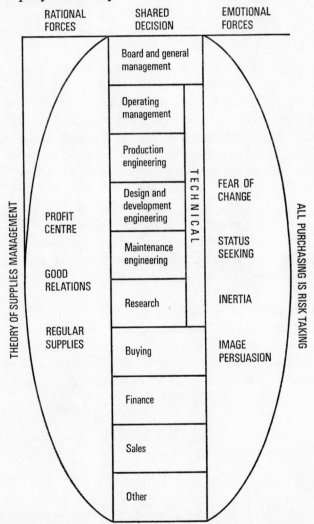

Figure 8 Industrial purchasing behaviour, rational and emotional forces

8

The Sales Approach in Industrial Marketing

The acceptance of the marketing mix concept with its emphasis on the co-ordination of the marketing functions has led, in recent years, to the development of sophisticated techniques of sales forecasting, new product planning, pricing, media evaluation, distribution analysis and models of market behaviour. To be complete, however, any progress in the development of the marketing mix must include the efficient use of the longest established of all marketing functions, the meeting of salesman and customer.

A distinction can be made between the use of effective selling techniques per se and the use of the sales force within the promotional mix. The first is a matter of sales training and the second is the responsibility of marketing management in understanding how a suitable marketing climate to support that selling effort should be created.

To assist individual managers in their interpretation of the results of research into industrial purchasing behaviour the following check lists have been prepared. The topics raised by the questions posed provide an opportunity for the evaluation of existing sales approaches and an examination of the extent to which the operation of the sales force is related to marketing strategy.

CHECK LISTS

IMPLICATIONS FOR SALES TRAINING

First-time purchases

The research into industrial purchasing processes has confirmed the importance of 'getting in' early. If a high proportion of calls made are following up requests for information the sales force is missing out on the very early stages of the decision to purchase.

The efficiency of the sales force in this type of selling can be improved through training. Questions to be asked include the following:

Is the sales representative trained to:

1. Introduce himself to potential customer companies?
2. Ask questions which highlight customer problems?
3. Locate decision makers?
4. Locate decision influencers?
5. Adapt the sales approach to different interests of different decision makers?
   - product performance
   - product reliability
   - ease of operation
   - cost benefits

Does the sales representative use information on customers and customers' markets to:

1. Anticipate customer problems?
2. Recognise customer problems?
3. Persuade customer to recognise problems?
4. Identify potential applications for his product?
5. Decide what customer regards as *his* most important problem?
6. Translate product features into customer benefits?

Is the sales representative trained to:

1. Present technical information as a means of problem solving?
2. Recognise when additional technical support is required?
3. Act as liaison between customer and technical support service?
4. Refer to company's reputation for technical competence?
5. Reduce buying risk by providing proof of technical competence?
6. Keep Buyer informed of dealings with customer technical personnel?

When a technical solution to customer's problem is found, is the sales representative sufficiently skilled to:

1. Recognise what the Buyer regards as the most important benefit,
   — price
   — continuity of supply
   — delivery
   — method of payment
   — accessibility of supplier personnel.
2. Stress non-price advantages?
3. Ease communication between Buyer and supplier sales office?

Change of Supplier

Where a change is contemplated in the supplier of products of known and accepted technical performance, the Buyer is the most active and most influential member of the Decision Making Unit.

To gain new business from companies dissatisfied with the performance of their existing suppliers, is the sales representative trained to:

1. Concentrate his sales approach on the Buyer?
2. Recognise source of Buyer's dissatisfaction?
3. Stress relevant commercial features?
   — delivery
   — service
   — maintained quality.
4. Supply information to reduce risk of change to new supplier?
5. Facilitate evaluation by potential customer of product offered?
6. Maintain regular contact?
7. Recognise opportunities for change?
   — change in customer markets
   — new product development
   — change of purchasing personnel.

(Substantial changes in technical specification required would normally lead to the purchase being treated as a 'new purchase'.)

Repeat Purchases

The volume of purchases and the heavy involvement of leading members of the Decision Making Unit in new and modified purchasing decisions result in the delegation of repeat purchasing to purchasing staff acting on instructions as to the required specification and approved supplier previously agreed when the purchase was new to the company.

A sales representative can retain repeat business if he is able to maintain the status quo and thus prevent the re-purchase from coming under review as a modified purchase. His performance will improve if an affirmative answer can be given to the following check questions.

Is the sales representative trained to:

1. Call regularly on the customer company?
2. Maintain regular contact with both user department and purchasing personnel?
3. Anticipate changes in customer procedures, products, markets?
4. Feedback information relating to change?
5. Facilitate customer re-ordering?
6. Supply regular information on deliveries, prices, product improvements?
7. Give reasons for any deficiency in service or performance?
8. Rectify any customer dissatisfaction?
9. Assure customer of maintained technical competence?

A Check List for Marketing Management

1. How do you classify your product?
    — by type of product (capital equipment, raw material, component)
    — by type of purchasing situation (new purchase, change of supplier, repeat purchase)
2. Is the same 'sales package' offered for all purchasing situations?
3. Is the sales force supplied with information on customer industry?
    — manufacturing problems
    — market conditions
4. Are systems introduced to feedback market information?
5. Is such market information used to plan marketing strategy?
6. Is the sales force work load balanced to permit time for
    — new customer prospecting
    — familiarisation with customer industry problems?

7. Is sales remuneration geared to marketing priorities?
   — obtaining new customers
   — concentration on most profitable products
   — maximising revenue
8. Is specific advertising tuned to marketing priorities?
   — gaining new inquiries
   — stressing product advantages
   — product awareness
   — good delivery
   — competitive pricing
   — service follow up
9. Is the sales force supported by general 'image' or reputation advertising?
10. Is marketing strategy fully explained to the sales force?

IMPLICATIONS FOR SELLING

A great deal of training literature has been produced on sales techniques and the secrets for sales success, but little detailed study has been made of what happens in the sales process or how any rules of selling may be adapted to the varying circumstances of the industrial selling situation.

In 1969, the Institute of Marketing filled a gap in the information on sales management practice, by publishing a report prepared by Stuart Dunkeld entitled *Salesmen Under the Microscope*.[1] The report, based on the analysis of the returns in a postal survey from over 3,000 members of the Institute who had charge of salesmen, provided a number of facts on how salesmen are recruited, trained, motivated and rewarded. Included among the questions of fact were also some requesting the opinions of sales managers. One of these asked the respondents what they considered to be the difference in performance between their most successful salesman and their average salesman.

A list of differentiating factors was offered on the questionnaire and the respondents were asked to select six, weighting their replies 6 : 1, so that a total score was obtained providing an indication of the relative importance of the factors, or reasons chosen.

---

[1] Dunkeld, S. B., *Salesmen Under the Microscope*, Institute of Marketing, London 1969.

The results for industrial goods were as follows:

TABLE 7

REASONS FOR THE DIFFERENCE

The most successful salesman—	Repeat industrial goods	Capital equipment
has superior territory organisation	6th	6th
can obtain more interviews	10th	10th
makes a better initial impression	9th	9th
asks questions and listens more carefully	5th	4th
has greater product knowledge	1st	1st
makes a more enthusiastic presentation	2nd	2nd
answers objections better	8th	7th
has more ability to clinch the order	3rd	3rd
has better contacts/friendships within the industry	7th	8th
pays closer attention to ensuring customers receive good service	4th	5th

No amplification of the sales manager's opinion of what makes a good salesman is given in the report but the headings as presented above provide an opportunity for relating the findings of the research into industrial purchasing behaviour to the training and operation of the sales force.

Each factor is taken in turn although the order has been altered slightly in order to fit more logically into the natural flow of the salesman-customer relationship.

HAS GREATER PRODUCT KNOWLEDGE

Personal representation forms the major part of the communication process between industrial supplier and industrial purchaser. One of the many advantages the salesman has over display advertising or direct mail is his ability to answer secondary questions raised by the buyer: 'Yes, that is all very interesting, but will it fit our needs here?' 'You see we are in a very *special* line of business. . . .'

To answer this question the sales representative will need to know much more than the details of his own product or service, but if he is deficient in product knowledge he cannot begin to move the conversation in the right direction, even though more specialist technical advice may be required at a later date. A reply such as 'I'm sorry—I don't know—but I'll find out for you' seriously reduces the efficiency of the two way flow of information between buyer and seller—essential for a satisfactory sale. In representing his company and his company's product, the salesman provides the only reason the buyer is interested in him, namely, the benefits he (the buyer) can obtain from doing business with his company. It is not surprising, therefore, that a sales manager having committed himself to the expense of getting his salesman to the customer, does not want to frustrate the relationship between buyer and seller through the lack of basic information. Cyril Hudson, in a survey carried out with the co-operation of the Institute of Purchasing and Supply[3] revealed that 80 per cent of a sample of 427 buyers expected the representative to have complete product knowledge and 35 per cent expected salesmen to provide an expert value analysis of their propositions. Basic product knowledge, supported by application engineering where necessary, is the least that the buyer expects and it is the responsibility of the sales manager to see that his expectations are met.

New Purchases

The most important function of the industrial sales representative in the new purchase situation is to provide information, both technical and commercial, presented in such a way that it will assist the solution of the problem in question and improve the relationship between the customer company's technical and purchasing personnel (*Figure 9*).

[3] Hudson, C., *Professional Salesmanship*, Staple Press, London 1967.

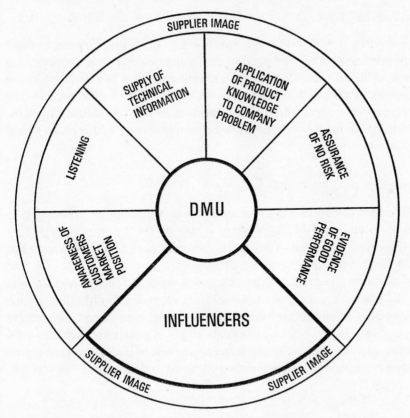

Figure 9 Role of the Sales Representative in New Purchase Decision

Repeat Purchases

If the purchase is being treated by the customer as a repeat purchase, however, the supplier's sales representative will need to rely less on his product knowledge in order to maintain his position. The product details will have been cleared at the new purchase stage and the technical personnel involved will have moved on to new problem areas. There exists a certain inertia in the technical area which springs from a combination of the reasonable view that changes in design and production methods are costly with the less demanding attitude of leaving well alone.

An attack on a repeat purchase supplier is most likely to come on the commercial front and to fend off such attacks the existing supplier must be in regular contact with the buyer in order to measure the strength of any competition and to keep the existing arrangement as smooth as possible.

Changing Suppliers

Similarly, a competitor supplier attempting to break in on a repeat purchase situation will need to assess any dissatisfaction experienced on technical grounds with the existing equipment or material in use before planning his approach. If there is little difference in the performance or quality of his product he will be wasting his time talking about the product to a buyer concerned with non-technical matters.

Applied Product Knowledge

Those involved in the purchasing decision process are interested in those details of the suppliers products or services which help them solve their problems. They are not interested in products as such but in what products will do for them.

A sales representative will be more successful if he can combine the knowledge of his own company's products with that of his customer's product, manufacturing processes and competitive position. This requires a translation of product characteristics into customer benefits, a topic referred to below under the heading of other important characteristics required by industrial sales representatives.

Makes a More Enthusiastic Presentation

The importance given by sales managers to the ability of their salesmen to make an enthusiastic presentation is understandable as there is a strong tendency for enthusiasm from the presenter of the product being offered to be taken up by the listener or buyer and communicated in turn by him to other members of the Decision Making Unit. Successful selling is not selling 'at' a customer but a process through which a potential customer is put into a state of mind or mood which will lead him to buy from the salesman.

Talking About His Problems

Products or services are purchased to solve problems and the representative who can detect the different problems facing different members of the DMU at different stages of the purchasing process will spend his time with customers more profitably than one who is frustrated in the initial task of creating interest.

Selling Skill

The results of the experimental research conducted by Levitt at the Harvard Business School showed that groups of engineers, designers and chemists were more favourably impressed by the selling company's image than the skill of the individual representative in presenting his product. The professional buyers, however, were more prepared to take notice of the presentation given by the representative trained in sales skills regardless of his company's reputation. One interpretation of Levitt's finding is that large companies with products backed by large resources and extensive research can 'get by' with mediocre salesmen, but as access to the customer's technical DMU members is most likely to be gained through the professional buyer, selling skill is necessary in any case.

Sales representatives are normally absent from the early stages of the decision to make new purchases but are then called in to give assistance when the details of the purchase are to be settled. In such a case where the customer is buying, rather than being influenced to start a purchase not previously thought of, the representative is soon past the buyer and presenting his product knowledge to the technical personnel involved. The more able he is to convince those influencing purchases at these early stages that he has the best solution to their problems, the less influence the professional buyer has on the selection of other potential suppliers at later stages of the process.

Selling skill however, is most important when an 'out' supplier is attempting to obtain a share of an 'in' suppliers' regular business because in such a case the professional buyer is most likely to be the key initiator of any change.

Asks Questions and Listens More Carefully

The majority of representatives are trained, either on the territory or during short courses, to ask questions. In order to make his sales contact with the right personnel and to select the most relevant approach, the sales representative needs to absorb a great deal of information about his customer. If he is called in to meet a particular need then the questions could be restricted to the job in hand, including such details as size, quantities, capacity, tolerance and performance. An opportunity usually exists, however, for the representative to be far more creative in his approach by suggesting alternative plans for action which would be more profitable to both buyer and seller.

Knowledge inspires the confidence which makes a creative sales approach possible. The knowledge required goes beyond the product knowledge discussed above to an awareness of the customers problems in his own markets.

An industrial sales representative can supply benefits through his product or service on two levels. First, there is the benefit of solving current problems, for example of production, design, or employee relations which, if not solved, would lead eventually to unprofitable operations. Secondly there is the more creative role of improving customer profitability by pointing out benefits in goods and services not previously realised by the customer.

Table 8 shows the range of knowledge required by an industrial sales representative to do his job efficiently. Some of this knowledge, such as manufacturing methods, testing procedures or stock holding policy, he can gain by asking questions and listening to the buyer's replies. A representative as a visitor to his customers' premises cannot spend the whole time asking questions, however, and he will need support from his own head office if he is to be kept up to date with the customer's competitive situation and other wide ranging developments impacting on his customers markets. A salesman on his territory can himself be a source of market intelligence but he does not have the time to carry out market research in the normally accepted sense of unbiased market information collected and interpreted by a specialist detached from the day-to-day needs of servicing individual customer's requirements.

TABLE 8

INFORMATION REQUIRED BY THE INDUSTRIAL SALES REPRESENTATIVE

Product Knowledge
        current specifications
        changes in performance
        new applications

        product benefits to buyer
        unique characteristic of product

Customer Knowledge
>   manufacturing methods
>   testing procedures
>   quality requirements
>   purchasing procedures
>   decision patterns
>   stockholding policy
>   need for technical advice
>   seasonality of demand
>   investment plans
>   product development plans
>   competitive situation (of customer)

Competitor Knowledge
>   who are the competitors, size and markets
>   competitor products, performance
>   marketing methods
>   advertising
>   types of salesmen

Sales Techniques
>   approaches to create interest
>   recognising what the buyer considers important
>   overcoming objections
>   closing the sale

Has More Ability to Clinch the Order

Industrial sales representatives have been known to react unfavourably to the topic of 'closing the sale' in formal training programmes. They have protested that closing techniques are more applicable to the training of the consumer goods salesman who may well be in a position to open and close a sale in one encounter with the customer whereas the industrial sale may take up to eighteen months.

This objection is based partly on the industrial salesman's dislike of being considered similar to the consumer salesman and partly on the facts borne out by the current research. The fact that industrial purchasing is a process effected through a variety of stages is indisputable even though some of these stages are telescoped in repeat and sometimes modified purchasing situations. During the purchasing process, decisions taken at an earlier stage influence the decisions possible at the later stages. The sales representative, therefore, is gradually preparing a situation which will lead to his obtaining the final order throughout the whole of his contact with the various members of the Decision Making Unit. He is 'closing the sale' all the way through.

Overcoming Objections

In the previous section the value of asking questions was discussed. In the answers to the questions posed the representative will not only collect the information he needs to direct his selling sequence but will also hear the objections raised by the buyer against the sale.

The contents of these objections are well worth listening to as they betray which factors, delivery, price, reliability, service, are considered to be important by the particular customer in question. If the sales representative can overcome these objections he will retain the interest of those influencing the purchase decision and be well on the way to clinching the sale.

All Purchasing is Risk Taking

Through his objections the buyer is expressing what he considers to be the risk involved in taking a positive purchasing decision. An important consideration here is Jacqueline Marrian's concept of the 'degree of essentiality'. If the product in question, for example, is a raw material forming a large or otherwise essential part of the company's purchases, then the buyer risks a great deal if he decides to change from the material currently used and technically acceptable to the product of a new supplier. Similarly, the apparent benefit of the lowest price for new equipment required has to be weighed against the risk of late delivery, poor performance or poor after sales service.

Obtaining the Order

The process of obtaining an order begins, at the early stages of the purchasing decision as the sales representative presents these benefits of his products or service related to the needs of the prospective purchaser. The objections raised during these discussions will guide the representative to the technical problems to be solved. If he, or his supporting engineers, can overcome the objections in these early technical stages the sale will move beyond its 'centre of gravity' to a successful completion if the commercial aspects of the product, its price, delivery terms, etc., are not too divorced from those offered by the competition. During the purchasing process the sales representative must isolate what are perceived to be the risk areas and supply 'information' which will reduce that risk.

A high level of risk is present in the new purchase as by definition the product or service is untried. This form of risk can be reduced by means of 'reference selling' by which the experience of buyers in other companies is offered by the sales representative as proof of his claims for the product. A strong image for research and development will help reduce the risk experienced by engineers and technical staff when recommending a new component or equipment.

Risk is also high where a change in supplier is being considered. If the technical risk is too high no change will take place but even when the technical problems are solved risk is present in the disturbance of change and the fear of being let down in one way or another. As in the new purchase, reference to other buyers will help overcome objections, but if the buyer is interested in bringing about the changes, he will seek out this 'reference' information from buyers in other companies on his own volition without being invited to do so.

Ensuring Customers Receive Good Service

It is dangerous to assume that 'good service' is a set of post purchase procedures or facilities offered by the supplier to all customers regardless of the particular purchasing situation involved.

When a company is purchasing a product for the first time, the sales representative should recognise that the main service he can offer is the provision of technical information relating to his product presented in such a way that it may be easily absorbed into the customer's problem solving activities.

During his contact with the Buyer in the new purchase situation the representative must be able to recognise what his customer really wants in the form of commercial service. It is assumed that prompt delivery is part of good service but the Buyer may be more concerned with the continuity of supply after the initial delivery has been made and here the best service the representative can provide is proof that the production capability exists and that his company has a reputation for not leaving its customers in the lurch in this way. In the construction industry examples referred to in Appendix B, the Buyer or Buying Committee show concern at the possibility of overloading a supplier of raw material who might then default some months after the building project had commenced.

In another context, for example, the installation of new plant or equipment, the technical or production members of the DMU may be interested in delivery dates but other members may be more concerned with the extent and terms of payment offered by the supplier.

In the repeat purchase situations, the emphasis shifts more to the traditional role of ensuring that customers continue to receive the service in terms of delivery, quality regularity of supply, technical support, promised at the new purchase stage. Ensuring that customers are sufficiently prepared for price increases is further example of customer service. The Buyer's determination to drop his existing supplier of printed circuit boards (Company *D*, pages 54–55) in favour of a new supplier resulted not only from the size of the price increase but from the suddenness of its announcement.

Where a change of supplier is contemplated, a representative can provide service by understanding the reasons for the change and by attempting to meet the terms and conditions required by the Buyer. In the more difficult task of getting a Buyer to change, the representative has first to discover whether the better service he can offer in price, delivery, credit, etc., is in fact regarded as 'better' or even thought of at all by the relevant members of the Decision Making Unit.

Superior Territory Organisation

An industrial sales force can be deployed by regional territories, customer industries or by product line and within these broad classifications the representatives' availability may be divided into units of time which in turn may be allocated proportionately in relation to a customer's existing or potential turnover.

The current research has shown the uniformity of the buying approach across a variety of manufacturing industries and this could be interpreted as support for the regional or territorial deployment of the sales force able to serve any number of customer industries located in his area.

There is, however, another research finding to be considered—that of the reliance of technical decision makers in customer companies on the sales representative as a key information source. To establish a profitable relationship, the sales representative must be able to apply his product knowledge to the particular needs of customers, but this may be too comprehensive a task if there are a number of industries to cover.

The decision as to the most profitable deployment of the sales representatives of one particular company cannot be based on these findings alone. More detailed information, normally available from a full scale market survey taking into account company resources, market structure, the needs of customers and competitor activity, is required before any final decision can be made.

FIGURE 11

RELATION OF RESEARCH KNOWLEDGE TO THE SALES APPROACH

Research Knowledge	*Sales Approach*
DMU concept TASK concept	Ask questions Listen to find out what is relevant to each DMU member
New Purchase—'information hunger' Change Supplier—commercial dissatisfaction Repeat Purchase—preferred list	—provide information —concentrate on commercial factors —regular calling
COMMUNICATIONS Technical Buyer EFFECTS Non-Technical Buyer	—Stress technical 'image' —Good sales presentation
ALL PURCHASING IS RISK TAKING INERTIA	Reduce risk through *validated* information Provide outside references Provide guarantees of competence Carry out promises Encourage visits to other customer installation Encourage favourable WOM contact Sell the Benefits
BUYER AS STATUS SEEKER	Keep Buyer informed of progress with Technical Decision taken
INCREASE POWER/INFLUENCE OF PROFESSIONAL BUYER	Relate benefits to customer industry problems. Knowledge of customer markets Stress 'profit centre' aspect of purchasing role

General Conclusion

The industrial sales task is a process of operations which, to be successful, must be matched to the series of decision stages constituting the customer's buying process.

An understanding of customer buying processes is not limited to a knowledge of procedures or even to an awareness of the Decision Making Unit. A full exploitation of the well-known facility of empathy, long recognised as a principle of successful selling is required to enable the sales representative to move from a fixed attitude as a supplier say of raw materials, components or even capital equipment, to a point where he can see the purchase from the buyer's point of view.

This demands a high degree of adaptability as the representative changes his approach to cater for the less formalised needs of a Decision Making Unit tackling his product as a first time purchase in contrast to the more defined requirements of a DMU changing supplier or making regular repeat purchases.

The more specific relationship between the Knowledge of Purchasing Behaviour and the sales approach is shown in *Figure 11*.

Appendix A

SURVEY METHOD

The survey, jointly sponsored by Industrial Market Research Ltd and the Institute of Marketing, was conducted by the author assisted by seven post-graduate students attending the Advanced Marketing Diploma course at the Bristol Polytechnic.

Approaches were made to 60 companies and organisations each employing over 250 personnel. Of these 43 gave permission for a researcher to trace the purchasing decisions relating to three or more specific products and to interview personnel involved in that process.

A total of 232 semi-structured personal interviews were conducted in the period October 1970–July 1971. A prompt card showing suggested stages of the purchasing process (see page 22) was shown to respondents to facilitate replies to a short check-list of questions but the objective of the inquiry, tracing past events, was found in pilot interviews to be most successfully achieved through a combination of semi-structured and totally unstructured interviews.

A further 20 unstructured interviews were conducted with industrial sales and marketing managers to discuss the preliminary findings and their application.

The Standard Industrial Classifications followed closely those from which information was collected in the original *How British Industry Buys* survey with the addition of exploratory interviews in the Public Utility and Education sectors. The purchasing information collected from these sectors has not been incorporated within the reported findings which refer generally to manufacturing industries. It is hoped that a separate survey may be made to appraise the purchasing procedures in the public sector and their implications for industrial marketing.

The Standard Industrial Classifications of the firms interviewed are shown below. It should be noted that the intention was to interview a number of different firms in different industries within the resources of time and finance. The selection of firms presented is not intended to imply that it is in any way a representative sample.

S.I.C.	*Firms Interviewed*
Food, Drink & Tobacco	5
Metal Manufacture	1
Mechanical Engineering	7
Electrical Engineering	6
Vehicles	3
Metal Industries (NES)	2
Clothing & Footware	3
Paper & Printing	3
Other Manufacturing	3
Construction	4
Gas, Electricity & Water	2
Transport & Communications	1
Professional & Scientific	3
	—
	43

Appendix B

PURCHASING PROCESSES IN THE CONSTRUCTION INDUSTRY

The purchasing examples followed through by the researchers in the construction industry could not be fitted within the classifications found suitable for the other industries covered.

In particular, the distinction between regular repeat purchases, for example, of new materials and changes in the suppliers of those materials, becomes blurred by the practice of treating each construction contract as a separate entity for which specified quantities of materials or types of plant are required. This provides a series of opportunities for those influencing the supply function to regard the purchases for each contract as 'new' purchases or at least as purchases to be made under changed circumstances.

New Purchases

Among the many purchases made for each contract by Company A below, however, there were new materials and new products being purchased for the first time. These were introduced through the architects' specifications backed by the recommendations of a centralised Research and Development department providing advice on all aspects of new or improved products. In addition, the Ministry of Works Library was used as a source of information of new products.

Company A: Contracting:
General Description of Raw Material Purchasing Procedures

RECOGNITION
OF NEED TO
PURCHASE

The Purchasing and Supply Department draw up an order schedule based on the requirements of the contract to be serviced.

PLANNING TYPE
OF PRODUCT
REQUIRED AND
DETAILED
DESCRIPTION OF
PURCHASES

The order schedule discussed at a meeting of the Buyer, Estimator, Accountant and Senior Administrative Officers.

The specifications are set by the Architects requirements although some latitude is generally permissible.

SEARCH FOR
POTENTIAL
SUPPLIERS

Suppliers normally contact Company *A* once it has been announced that a contract has been won. Files are kept giving technical information on products used on previous occasions but a great deal of similar information sent in by unknown suppliers is thrown away.

QUALIFICATION
OF SUPPLIERS
AND EVALUATING
PROPOSALS

This task is delegated by the Buyer to Section Leaders specialising in certain products. Quotations are examined in great detail and the suppliers evaluated to ensure that they are financially stable and capable of fulfilling their claims. Care is taken not to overload suppliers.

FEEDBACK-
SUPPLIER
EVALUATION

Reports are issued within the company on supplier performance. A supplier rated financially unstable or giving poor service on a maximum of three occasions will not be used again.

SELECTION
OF SUPPLIER

The selection of the supplier is made by the Section leader assisted by his staff. Delegation is necessary as up to 100 orders are handled daily. The relatively strict criteria on which quotations are evaluated may eliminate the lowest price quotation. In many instances 'trusted' suppliers will receive orders automatically.

Company B: Civil Engineering:
General Description of Raw Material Purchasing Procedures

RECOGNITION
OF NEED TO
PURCHASE

A tender is submitted by Company *B* to the firm of consultants advising a Local Authority requiring construction work.

PLANNING TYPE
OF PRODUCTS
REQUIRED

At the pre-tender stage a panel meets to discuss the products and materials required. The panel includes the Chief Estimator, the Buyer, Chief Engineer, Planning Manager, Contracts Manager and the Quantity Surveyor.

PREPARING
DETAILED
DESCRIPTION OF
PURCHASES

The Chief Estimator with a staff of eight estimators prepare the detailed descriptions. When awarding the contract, the consultants will frequently specify the materials to be used, and the name of the preferred supplier.

SEARCH FOR
POTENTIAL
SUPPLIERS

Junior staff draw up details of potential suppliers, prices and discounts offered. The site location may restrict the number of possible suppliers for a specified raw material to two or three firms. If money on the contract is 'tight' the purchasing staff may look further afield to up to six potential suppliers. Representatives and more senior executives of supplying firms call on the Buyer. Search is also made in Kelly's Directory and to a lesser extent, Sell's Directory. Direct Mail advertising is not judged to be an important aid in the search for suppliers.

EVALUATING
SUPPLIER
QUOTATIONS

The Buyer evaluates the standing and performance of suppliers. He settles a price to be paid taking the advantage of a lower price supplier than the one recommended by the consultants where the clause 'or other approved suppliers' is included in the specification details.

SELECTION OF THE
SUPPLIER/AND
ORDER ROUTINE

When the Buyer has settled the price to be paid and has put forward his views on which suppliers are to be preferred, the task of arranging delivery from particular suppliers is delegated to the Site Agent.

COMMENTS ON CONSTRUCTION EXAMPLES

Although different in many respects from the other examples quoted from manufacturing industry, certain similarities are present which confirm important features of the industrial purchasing process.

In both examples the heavy work load involved in the preparation of detailed buying specifications limits the effort available for a thorough search for new sources of supply. This results in a 'buying inertia' which favours those well-known suppliers who have established dependable reputations through previous contact. A further point which has evolved from the analysis of repeat purchase procedures in other industries, is the influence of junior members of Buying department on the final selection of suppliers for a preferred list previously approved by the Buyer or other senior members of the Decision Making Unit.

Appendix C

PURCHASING AT FORD

A description of company purchasing objectives and procedures has been published by the Educational Affairs Department, Ford Motor Company, Dearborn, Michigan. An extract is reproduced here with permission, as an example of a highly structured approach in purchasing management.

The automotive industry is the largest of the durable goods industries. It is also one of the biggest customers in American business, spending more than $25,000 every minute of the year. The effect of the automotive industry as a purchaser is felt throughout the economy. Many thousands of companies supply it with the parts, raw materials, tools and other equipment needed for the complex business of putting America on wheels.

Automobile manufacturing ranks first in the consumption of materials by an individual industry. It is the largest single consumer of steel, with purchases of roughly 20 per cent of total steel shipments. It buys some 60 per cent of all the synthetic rubber produced, consumes 60 per cent of the lead mined in this country, and uses 72 per cent of plate glass and 55 per cent of iron production.

In addition, enormous quantities of aluminum, copper, zinc, machine tools and chemicals are required to make automobiles. American automobile companies are also high-volume customers of service organisations, such as the electric and water utilities and the various transportation industries.

Not only is the industry first in the consumption of materials, it is also a leader in employment and total payroll. For every employee directly engaged in automotive manufacturing, there are several additional workers in the plants of suppliers. This pyramids the number of jobs and also accelerates the influx of supplier dollars into the economy. The effect of a single automotive purchasing dollar entering trade channels is multiplied four or five times.

The growth of the automotive industry has resulted in a similar expansion of the firms that supply it. The great variety and specialised nature of the supplier firms have enabled the automotive industry to remain flexible despite the tendency of mass production to result in inflexibility. If the industry had to produce all of the thousands of specialised parts it now purchases from outside suppliers, its already heavy investment in tools, machines and facilities would have to be increased enormously.

There is constant change in the type and quantity of items purchased by the automotive industry. Today's cars contain far greater proportions of aluminum, plastics, galvanised steel and vinyl than cars of only a decade ago. Even the use of such a staple item as steel fluctuates with changes in car design.

Almost two thirds of every dollar of cost in automobile manufacture is a purchased cost. An increase in such costs of only pennies, when multiplied by the enormous number of units produced by the industry, can mount up to a staggering figure. Purchasing personnel are responsible for avoiding every penny of purchased cost that does not give value to the customer.

The role of purchasing is vital to the automotive industry. Purchasing operations at Ford Motor Company, one of the world's largest automobile manufacturers, illustrate the many varied ways in which purchasing helps eliminate unnecessary costs while providing the utmost car value.

OBJECTIVES OF PURCHASING

The primary job of Purchasing in the procurement cycle is to locate suppliers who can deliver all items in the required quantity, at the required time and according to specifications, and to purchase such items at a competitive price.

Another major function of Purchasing is cost analysis—the determination of how much raw materials, tooling and manufactured parts *should* cost.

The over-all objectives of Purchasing can be listed as follows:

(1) To buy parts, materials and supplies of required quality.
(2) To assure adequate capacity and capability for the supply and delivery of material at scheduled times.
(3) To obtain the lowest cost on all purchases in keeping with quality and delivery requirements and at the same time give efficient suppliers fair profits.
(4) To establish and maintain good relationships with suppliers, encouraging their suggestions, advice and assistance in improving both the Company's products and their own.
(5) To conduct all purchasing activities in such a way as to build and maintain good community, public, supplier and employee relations.
(6) To develop and maintain strong, well-qualified staffs of Purchasing personnel for the Central Staff and the divisions.
(7) To work closely with other organisational components of the Company in improving the product and lowering costs.

PROCUREMENT

Ford Motor Company spends more than five billion dollars a year buying thousands of different items and services from some 25,000 independent domestic suppliers, while approximately two billion dollars is spent annually by Ford subsidiaries around the world. More than half of the approximately 15,000 parts that go into the making of a single car are purchased from outside suppliers, and more than 100,000 production and non-production items must be bought to support manufacturing operations. All of these must be of high quality and must be purchased at a price that will allow the Company to produce its vehicles economically.

At Ford, Purchasing is assigned responsibility for selecting suppliers, for negotiation with suppliers, for making final contractual commitments and for the evaluation of supplier performance. Purchasing, Traffic and Production Control share responsibility for providing follow-up and expediting services.

Commodities—Basically, the Ford purchasing organisation is set up to take advantage of commodity specialisation. There are five broad commodity classifications:

> Raw Materials (for basic manufacture, such as steel, foundry and glass operations)
> Experimental, Research and Styling Materials (for research and product development)
> Production and Service Parts (for manufacture, assembly and service)
> Facilities (machinery, equipment, tools and construction)
> Non-Production and Operating Supplies (miscellaneous materials and services needed for varied operations)

Selection of Suppliers

Purchasing personnel attempt to match the Company's procurement requirements with available or potential sources of supply. To do this successfully, the buyer must first familiarise himself with the blueprints and specifications of the parts to be purchased.

Next, he checks the sources available or, if there are none, he attempts to develop suppliers capable of producing the required parts. While developing new suppliers, he may be required to undertake studies of the parts involved or of the industry that can make them.

Adequacy of the supplier's physical facilities is a crucial consideration. The buyer may ask qualified technicians to visit a prospective supplier's plant and determine its capacity to do the required job. He may also obtain an evaluation of the managerial capabilities of the supplier's personnel, as well as his business reputation and record of financial responsibility.

After determining that a supplier meets these requirements, the buyer must determine whether that supplier's price will be competitive. To do this, he solicits written quotations from three or more qualified sources. If such sources are not available, the buyer will take appropriate action to qualify additional ones. He uses target prices established by the purchase analysis department to evaluate the quoted prices if the item is a 'key part'.

The buyer uses all of the information he has to select the supplier who can best meet Company requirements on quality, delivery and price.

The qualified bidder submitting the lowest price quotation is usually awarded the contract. When competitive quotations cannot be obtained or an award is made to other than the lowest bidder, appropriate management approvals for such action are obtained.

Purchase Commitments

Whenever a purchase is made, a written document containing the details of the transaction is prepared. Depending on the type of item or service purchased, the written document will be one of the following types:

Purchase Orders—Various kinds of purchase orders exist, each with appropriate terms and conditions that apply to the specific type of commodity or service.

Construction Contracts—Contracts for major construction and installation projects include plans, specifications and general conditions under which the work is to be undertaken.

Special Contracts—In some instances where purchase orders are not appropriate, as in the buying of certain basic raw materials, a special contract is drafted.

Letters of Intent—Preliminary contracts are used when sufficient information is not available to prepare one of the documents described above and it is necessary to permit a supplier to start work or purchase materials he requires. Letters of intent are replaced by purchase orders, construction contracts or special contracts when all details are agreed upon.

Quantity

Engineering specifications describe the *type* of manufactured parts or materials which are to be produced. Production Control then calculates the *quantity* of each item and establishes parts requirements for the model year. Purchasing negotiates 'blanket order' contracts for most production parts. Blanket orders set a percentage of Company requirements that can be bought periodically at the negotiated price over a specified period of time—usually one year. Production Control simply 'releases' or specifies a certain quantity against the blanket orders sufficient to meet the established production schedules.

DETERMINATION OF MANUFACTURING FEASIBILITY

When parts are purchased from an outside supplier rather than from within the Company, the Company requests the supplier's opinion as to whether the parts can be made with existing equipment according to Company specifications. Each supplier is encouraged to make contributions that help improve Company products and processes. Purchasing asks suppliers to submit quotations subject to the following conditions:

'If you cannot meet the referenced blueprints or specifications in any particular, you must advise the buyer before submitting your quotation.

'Further, if the blueprints or specifications are likely in any way to cause manufacturing problems or affect adversely the quality of the part or assembly, you should also advise the buyer before submitting your quotation.'

These conditions are extremely important to a supplier, since Purchasing insists that he meet the specifications in every respect after he has accepted a purchase order.

Measuring Supplier Performance

Several programmes have been developed by Ford Purchasing to measure the performance of outside suppliers:

Initial Samples—Before beginning volume production, each supplier must provide samples demonstrating his ability to produce parts meeting specifications. The supplier's inspection and testing of these samples are verified by a Ford Quality Control representative.

Special Durability Testing—In the case of certain functional parts, specifications will include durability tests over and above regular dimensional and material requirements. Suppliers of such parts must conduct these tests and certify that the parts have performed satisfactorily.

Warranty Expenses—One measure of the success of the Company and its suppliers in maintaining the high quality of Ford products is provided by warranty expenses. These are the amounts of money that are paid by the Company to its dealers for corrective work performed on their customers' new cars over a specified period of time. This information becomes a major consideration in evaluating supplier performance.

International Procurement

Purchasing activities at Ford Motor Company's numerous manufacturing and assembly operations abroad operate much the same as their domestic counterparts. They make many required purchases locally. In addition, all Company locations assist each other in finding sources of supply. For example, Ford of Britain will assist Ford of Germany or the domestic United States operations in finding suppliers in England. This type of cooperation was exemplified in the 'Redcap' programme, a joint undertaking by Ford of Britain and Ford of Germany. One identical type of light truck was being built by the two operations. Ford of Germany purchased some of the required parts in England, and vice versa.

PROCUREMENT IN A TYPICAL PURCHASING ACTIVITY

All purchasing activities in the divisional operations of Ford Motor Company follow the same general policies and employ the same procurement procedures.

Each Divisional Purchasing Office assists in a highly organised programme designed to control the cost of purchased materials for that division.

In addition to providing buyers with information on specific price changes resulting from design modifications or increased material costs, purchase analysts provide buyers with estimates of the target prices that should be paid for parts. Buyers are expected to use the target prices in negotiations with suppliers. They are also expected to be constantly alert to market availability of new materials, more economical processes and other ways to reduce costs.

Negotiations with Suppliers

The following Company policies guide all Ford Purchasing activities in negotiations with suppliers:

Supplier Relations—The suppliers are an integral part of the organisation required to produce Ford products. Their production and engineering abilities, their cooperation in solving difficult problems and their assistance during periods of emergency are of immeasurable value.

A Director of Purchasing Policy and Planning is available to assist in maintaining and promoting sound business relationships, based on mutual understanding and respect, between Ford and its suppliers.

Supplier Contributions—Purchasing encourages its suppliers to maintain progressive research and development facilities and to cooperate actively in the development and improvement of Company products.

Suppliers' research and development contributions are of such importance to the Company that Purchasing's handling of all phases of its relationships with suppliers should serve to encourage them to continue and increase their contributions. Certain principles have been established whose application to these relationships will assist in providing this encouragement.

Development—Purchasing arranges for timely and proper consideration by the appropriate Company activities of all suggestions and ideas submitted by suppliers. A supplier is assured that his competitive proposals will receive fair consideration.

Suppliers are directly and fairly compensated for research and development work performed at the request of the Company.

A supplier's research and development efforts in Ford's behalf, whether or not performed by request, are weighed in terms of significance to the Company, and the supplier is rewarded accordingly.

Buyers establish close liaison with Product Engineering in order to be fully informed with respect to contributions made by suppliers in their area of responsibility.

Price Negotiations—Suppliers may furnish significant engineering services in connection with the development, engineering and releasing of production parts and assemblies. In evaluating their quotations, recognition is given to this assistance, its value to the Company and the costs incurred by the suppliers in rendering it. For example, where such a change has resulted in the reduction of the cost of an item, the cost saving is shared with the supplier on a fair and equitable basis.

Continuity of Sourcing Arrangements—Continuity of sourcing, or the expectation of such continuity, can encourage the efficient and competitive supplier to improve his operations and performance. Accordingly, the Company tries to maintain stable sourcing relationships with its suppliers, consistent with good competitive practices, including the stimulation of new potential, because it provides mutual advantages both in the long and short run. These benefits may include a willingness on the part of suppliers:

(1) To devote more time and effort to research and development projects and to share with the Company new products, ideas or cost savings which may result.
(2) To assume additional risks and provide special services associated
    . with their products.

While maintaining sourcing continuity is a basic objective, it is recognised that instances will arise where there may be a substantial reason for changing sources. Examples of such reasons are:

Current Supplier:

(1) Has failed to meet fully the quality requirements despite efforts to effect corrective action.
(2) Has consistently failed to meet delivery requirements.
(3) Has experienced financial deterioration and does not have the working capital to carry the required raw material, in process and finished goods inventories.

Potential Supplier:

(1) Has made a significant research and development contribution in connection with the business being sourced.
(2) Has offered a significantly lower price.

In a resourcing decision, price advantage should not necessarily be the prime consideration. Not only should the price offered by a potential supplier be significantly lower than the current supplier, but other factors should be given consideration as well; for example, continuing the present sourcing relationship with a supplier who has unamortised unique facilities or facilities recently modernised or expanded to permit more efficient production of Company requirements. Other points evaluated in a Purchasing decision are: a supplier's long-standing service to the Company, financial impact on the supplier, Company costs incidental to source changes and the supplier's contributions to Company products or processes.

The final sourcing decision must include consideration of all pertinent factors and be based upon common sense and equity for both Company and suppliers.

Agents or Brokers—Contracts are usually made directly with suppliers, and not with agents or brokers. If negotiations are conducted with other than a direct representative of the supplier, the purchase order is issued to the company which will supply the item in question.

Company Plans—Company plans concerning production programmes and related supply requirements have a significant effect upon the plans, programmes and facility requirements of its suppliers. It is essential to the maintenance of good supplier relations and a sound supplier system that suppliers be advised in a timely manner of Company plans and decisions that may affect them.

Good Business Ethics—Good business ethics are guiding principles in all negotiations in order to maintain a continuing reputation of good community and supplier relations. Some of these principles are:

(1) One supplier's quotation is not disclosed to another.

(2) One supplier is not placed unfairly against another for purposes of reducing prices.

(3) The selection of suppliers ordinarily should be made on the basis of the original quotations. (If all quotes are excessive, it is, of course, appropriate to reject them and obtain new ones.)

(4) When soliciting quotations, a buyer shall neither imply the price necessary to obtain the business, nor reveal the relative competitive position of a supplier's original bid.

(5) After an award has been made, it is appropriate to advise an unsuccessful bidder that his price was not competitive and the area in which it was not competitive, but neither the price at which the business was awarded nor the quotations of other sources are revealed.

Competitive Prices—Realistic, competitive prices must be the basis for all purchases. Wherever possible, written quotations are obtained from at least three qualified suppliers. Where competitive bids cannot be obtained because of requirements relating to engineering approvals, patent restrictions, material standards, replacement parts or other reasons, the reason and justification for the decision is noted and made part of the purchase record. Awards are ordinarily made to the lowest qualified bidder.

PURCHASING HELPS CREATE A NEW MODEL

Development work on a new car starts years in advance of its introduction. It is the job of Product Development to anticipate, develop and test car designs that will be in demand four years or more in the future. While a final plan or program for the new cars is still being decided upon, Purchasing is often called in to advise the product planners on anticipated costs.

A cost-control programme is organised and budgeted. Control starts with a listing of all the materials required to build the automobile. This usually is a priced bill of materials for a current model similar to the new vehicle. Product planners review this list of materials. All parts that will not be used on the new model are eliminated. Preliminary cost estimates are then drafted on the new parts that will be required. This estimate (made even before drawings of the new model are available) is revised and refined until finally it becomes the budget that will guide the designers and engineers in their work on the new model.

This budget covers all of the basic elements of the new car—the engine, body, chassis, ornamentation, etc. As styling and engineering progress, cost estimates are continually updated. When it appears that the cost of a major component assembly is going to exceed the amount budgeted for it, the excess cost is brought to the attention of Product Development. The product planners then must either cut back on anticipated costs or convince management that the new car should cost more than the original estimate.

Mandatory Design Changes

As Job No. 1 (the first car off the assembly line) draws near, it becomes more difficult to make design changes. Despite rigorous testing, some changes in design may be mandatory, cost factors notwithstanding. As soon as possible, engineers assemble a handmade prototype car to test the basic mechanism of the new model. Any changes required as a result of this testing are subjected to a cost analysis by Purchasing.

When engineers begin testing the first pilot model made on a production line, some three months prior to Job No. 1, the problem of making design changes becomes very difficult. Although the final production vehicle will be identical to the pilot model in almost every detail, it is inevitable that some components in the pilot model will have to be modified.

If a change is required on the pilot model, Purchasing asks the parts supplier involved for an estimate of the retooling time needed. Because time is limited, suppliers must sometimes begin retooling before complete engineering information is available.

How Purchase Analysts Estimate Costs

An experienced Ford buyer can look at specifications for a new part and produce a very accurate cost estimate by comparing the new item with similar parts purchased in the past. Ford purchase analysts use this technique, but they also use far more sophisticated estimating methods that can provide even greater accuracy.

Purchase analysts estimate costs with the same basic methods used by cost estimators at supplier plants. They precisely compute the rough weight of material needed to make the part by studying the blueprint and allowing for extra material to accommodate the manufacturing process that will be used. Since they are familiar with the processes used in making the parts, they can estimate what equipment will be needed and the rate at which the operations will be performed. From this data, it is possible to calculate direct labour costs by multiplying the minutes of labour required by the prevailing wage rate. Analysts select overhead rates to apply to various types of products and manufacturing operations. Factory overhead is usually expressed as a percentage of direct labour costs. The labour and overhead estimates also include allowance for delays, set-up time, scrap, etc.

To the total production cost (labour, materials and overhead), analysts add estimated commercial and administrative expense and a profit allowance. The total becomes the estimated price. These estimates are the bases for management decisions, and buyers use them as target prices in negotiations.

Key Parts System—Purchasing's intensive cost control system is highly selective. By the inclusion of approximately 10 per cent of total vehicle end items in the sample of 'key parts' (controlled parts), control is possible on an average of 72 per cent of the dollar value of the purchased materials of major lines. All parts subject to frequent styling changes—for example, outside body mouldings—are classified as key parts regardless of price.

Along with such design cost estimates, purchase analysts also can forecast the effect of changes in labour rates or material costs, since the labour and material content of each key part is known.

For example, to find how much it would cost to make a car ten inches longer, purchase analysts can study the parts involved and provide an accurate estimate; or, they can predict the effect of a steel price increase on total vehicle cost by multiplying the steel content of the parts by the expected price increase.

Estimating Competitors' Costs—The cost estimating function is not limited to the Company's own production. Products made by competitors are purchased, disassembled and examined by a team of purchase analysts who estimate the cost of every component. Such cost estimating of competitive products provides valuable information to product planners and engineers.

Tooling Costs—In addition to controlling the cost of purchased parts, Purchasing spends an average of more than $100 million per year on required tooling. Normally, it issues a separate order for tooling to the supplier who makes the part. The supplier, in turn, may either make the tooling in his own shop or subcontract it to independent tool shops.

Tooling costs are controlled by a separate estimating section. Many of the personnel in this section are former toolmakers with years of experience in processing and tool cost estimating. As a result, they frequently are able to eliminate tooling costs through design or processing changes while reviewing the supplier's tool cost quotation.

ORGANISATION

Company Organisation

Ford Motor Company is organised according to the line-and-staff plan. Under this arrangement authority runs in a straight line from the head of the Company through intermediate executives and supervisors to the workman on the job. A group of specialists and technicians comprise a 'staff' that assists the head of the Company in discharging his responsibilities.

The Company is also organised into divisions, on a product or manufacturing process basis. The vehicle divisions are responsible for marketing the completed automobile (example: Ford Division). Manufacturing Divisions are responsible for major vehicle components (example: Transmission and Chassis Division). Other divisions produce items by specialised manufacturing processes (example: Steel Division).

Staff does not have direct supervision over the divisions, but it does prescribe policies and procedures that guide divisional management and it assists, also, in divisional programmes.

Appendix D

THE TASK APPROACH TO BUYING

Full description of the Buying Tasks as defined by Robinson & Faris.

New Task
- (a) need for the product has not risen previously.
- (b) little or no past buying experience is available to assist in the purchasing decision.
- (c) members of the buying unit require a great deal of information.
- (d) alternative ways of meeting the need are likely to be under review.
- (e) the situation occurs infrequently but the decisions taken may set a pattern for more routine purchases subsequently.
- (f) opportunities exist at an early stage in the decision process for external (marketing) inputs to have an influence on the final decision made.

Modified Rebuy
- (a) a regular requirement for the type of product exists.
- (b) the buying alternatives are known, but sufficient change has occurred to require some alteration to the normal supply procedure.
- (c) change may be stimulated by external events, e.g. inputs from supplying companies.
- (d) change may be stimulated by internal events, e.g. new buying influences, value analysis, re-organisation.

Straight Rebuy
- (a) routine purchasing procedures exist.
- (b) the buying alternatives are known but a formal or informal list of 'approved' suppliers is available.
- (c) no supplier not on the list is considered.
- (d) decision on each separate transaction is made by the purchasing department.
- (e) buyers have relevant buying experience and require little new information.

Bibliography

References for further reading supplementing Chapter 5, 'What Do We Know About Buyer Behaviour?'

ALEXANDER, J. O. M., 'The Role of the Supplies Function in Management', *Purchasing Journal*, London 1969.

AMES, B. CHARLES, 'Marketing Planning for Industrial Products', *Harvard Business Review*, September–October 1968.

AMMER, D. S., 'Materials Management as a Profit Center', *Harvard Business Review*, January–February 1969.

BAUER, R. A., 'Consumer Behavior as Risk Taking', *Proceedings 43rd Conference, American Marketing Assoc.* 1960.

BLOIS, K. J., 'The Effect of Subjective Factors on Customer/Supplier Relations', *British Journal of Marketing*, Spring 1970.

BUCKNER, H., *How British Industry Buys*, Hutchinson, London 1967.

CLOHESEY, J. E., 'The Polished Purchasers', *Sales Management* (US), August 1964.

COREY, E. R., *Industrial Marketing; Cases and Concepts*, Prentice Hall, 1962.

DUNCAN, D. J., 'What Motivates Business Buyers', *Harvard Business Review*, 1940.

COX, D. F. (ed.), *Risk Taking and Information Handling in Consumer Behavior*, Division of Research, Graduate School of Business Administration, Boston 1967.

ENGLAND, W., *Procurement: Principles and Cases*, 4th ed. R. D. Irwin, 1962.

FELDMAN, W. AND CARDOZO, R. W., 'Industrial Buying and Consumer Behavior or the Repressed Revolution', *American Marketing Association Proceedings*, June 1968.

HOWARD, J. A., *Marketing: Executive and Buyer Behavior*, Columbia University Press.

HUDSON, C. L., 'An Integrated Approach to the Buying-Selling Situation—a Trend Towards a Totality of Advantages Concept?' *Marketing World*, Vol. 1, No. 3, February 1970.

JAMES, B., 'Emotional Buying in the Industrial Market', *Scientific Business*, Spring 1966.

JOHNE, F. A., 'Supplier Evaluation Schemes Within the Context of the Industrial Marketing Transaction', *Marketing Forum*, January–February 1970, Inst. of Marketing, London.

KOTLER, P., 'Behavioral Models for Analizing Buyers', *Journal of Marketing* (US), Vol. 29, October 1965; also Chapter 4 of *Marketing Management: Analysis, Planning and Control*, Prentice-Hall, New Jersey 1967.

LAZO, H., 'Emotional Aspects of Industrial Buying', *American Marketing Association Proceedings*, June 1960.

LAZO, H. AND CORBIN, A., 'Sales as Part of Marketing' in *Management in Marketing: Texts and Cases*, N.Y. McGraw-Hill, 1961.

LEVITT, T., 'Marketing Myopia', *Harvard Business Review*, July–August 1960.

LEVITT, T., *Industrial Purchasing Behavior*, Division of Research, Graduate School of Business Administration, Boston, 1965.

MACAY, G. T., 'What Management Expects from a Purchasing Department', *Purchasing Journal*, London, June 1970.

MCPHERSON, J. H., 'Does the Purchasing Agent's Ego Get in the Way of his Job?' *Iron Age* (US), March 1966.

MONSEN, R. S. AND DOWNS, A., 'A Theory of the Large Managerial Firm', *Journal of Political Economy*, June 1965.

MARRIAN, J., 'Marketing Characteristics of Industrial Goods and Buyers' in Wilson, A. (ed.), *The Marketing of Industrial Products*, Hutchinson, London 1965; second edition Pan Books 1972.

RAYHER, W., 'Operating Management and Purchasing as a Team', *Management Review* (US), May 1971.

ROBERTSON, G. M., 'Motives in Industrial Buying', *American Marketing Association Proceedings*, June 1960.

ROWE, D. AND ALEXANDER, I., *Selling Industrial Products*, Hutchinson, London 1968.

ROBINSON, P. J., FARIS, C. W. AND WIND, Y., *Industrial Buying and Creative Marketing*, Allyn & Bacon, Boston, 1967.

SAWYER, H. G., 'What Does the Industrial Buyer's Emotional Involvement Mean to You?, *Industrial Marketing* (US), May 1959.

SHOAF, R. F., 'Here's Proof—The Industrial Buyer is Human', *Industrial Marketing* (US), May 1959.

STRAUSS, G., 'Tactics of Lateral Relationships: The Purchasing Agent', *Administrative Science Quartery*, VII, September 1962.

TOFTE, A. R., 'They Don't Buy Bulldozers the Way they Buy Beer', *Industrial Marketing* (US), March 1960.

WEBSTER, F. E., Jnr., 'Modelling the Industrial Buying Process', *Journal of Marketing Research*, November 1965.

WEIGAND, R. E., 'Why Studying the Purchasing Agent is not Enough', *Journal of Marketing*, Vol. 32, January 1968.

WEIGAND, R. E., 'Identifying Industrial Buying Responsibility', *Journal of Marketing Research*, Vol. III, February 1966.

WILSON, A., *Assessment of Industrial Markets*, Hutchinson, London 1969.

WILSON, A., 'The Art and Practice of Marketing', Chapter 8, *Researching Industrial Images*, Hutchinson, London 1971.

Index

Page references in italics indicate a table or a diagram